Memoir Upon The Late War In America, Between The French And English, 1755-60

Followed By Observations Upon The Theatre Of Actual War, And By New Details Concerning The Manners And Customs Of The Indians ; With Topographical Maps

(Volume II)

Pierre Pouchot, Hough Franklin Benjamin

Alpha Editions

This edition published in 2021

ISBN : 9789354489846

Design and Setting By
Alpha Editions
www.alphaedis.com
Email - info@alphaedis.com

MEMOIR

UPON THE

BETWEEN THE

FRENCH AND ENGLISH,

1755-60;

FOLLOWED BY

OBSERVATIONS UPON THE THEATRE OF ACTUAL WAR, AND BY NEW
DETAILS CONCERNING THE MANNERS AND CUSTOMS OF THE
INDIANS; WITH TOPOGRAPHICAL MAPS.

*Chevalier of the Royal and Military Order of St. Louis; former Captain of the
Regt. of Bearn; Commandant of Forts Niagara and Levis in Canada.*

TRANSLATED AND EDITED

BY

WITH ADDITIONAL NOTES AND ILLUSTRATIONS.

VOL. II.

PRINTED FOR W. ELLIOT WOODWARD,
ROXBURY, MASS.

MEMOIR UPON THE LAST WAR.

On the 27th of June, 1760, a Chouegatchi Indian
brought in an Onondaga from the Kenchiagé river.[1]
He was one of a party sent against us, composed of
three Senecas, two Cayugas, four Mohegans, two
negroes and an Englishman, with the son of Sonnonguires.   He announced a visit from the latter on
the morrow.   Our Indian related that the Mohegans
had done all they could to induce the others to take
his scalp, but that the Onondagas did not wish to do
this, representing that this was not necessary, as in
wars between Indians, that the whites were satisfied
with prisoners, from whom they could get news, that
they might give them something, and that therefore
they had let them go.   The two Onondagas came,
having relatives at La Presentation, and the remainder of the party were released.   We may judge
of their simplicity, as they thought they could tell us
something of their mission.

---

[1] Black river.— ED.

Our Loups who arrived from their war party, brought in two English prisoners, and one scalp. One was a militia captain, and the other his brother, who lived on the Mohawk river. M. Pouchot had lodged at their house when he was going down to New York, and they had not received him very well, and would scarcely admit him. The Indians had dressed and painted them after their manner. They were about six feet high, and they made them dance the chichicoy, the common dance of the slaves. This is an indispensable ceremony. They were very happy in escaping the ordinary beating, by coming directly upon the island to the quarters of M. Pouchot, who recognized them in the dance. This mortification did not absolutely humble them. They were directed to lodge in the quarters of the post surgeon, and sent to eat at his mess.

They informed us that General Amherst commanded the army, which was composed of eleven thousand men, who had much artillery, and that they were every day passing towards Oswego.

M. Pouchot also heard the son of Sonnonguires, who told him that all the Indians had sung for the war against the French, and that we would be threatened by them. The Five Nations had carried belts as far as to the Miamis, to engage all the nations to lay down the hatchet, and that they should be all reconciled among themselves. M. Pouchot questioned the truth of these statements, and replied; "See how your father is, he can never believe what the Indians say." He also said that there were only two regiments at Oswego, and that he did not know whether any more would come, as he was confused by the accounts of the English themselves.

On the 30th, Saoten arrived. He said that eight days before, he had left the Onondaga's village, that he had crossed the river near Oneida lake, that they had heard the strokes of oars along the river for twenty days, and that he had passed eight bands,[1] and eight chiefs. They were wagoning provisions constantly, and had a great many cannon, mortars and howitzers. He added that they said there were few people in the direction of St. Frederic, and that at the arrival of the army, the Iroquois and Mohegans were going to assemble at Oswego. According to his account, the English had made some large bateaux to carry forty men each, and a great cannon, and that while they did not wish to take but a little artillery, the Mohawks had advised them to take a great deal, because they might sink some of it in going down to Montreal.

He also told M. Pouchot, that the Onondaga chiefs to whom he had sent some strings to keep them quiet, had charged him to reply verbally and without formal words, but that they would not the least believe him. According to him, four great chiefs had deliberated together, to not allow their warriors to follow the

---

[1] Regiments.— *Note in Original.*

army, and that one of them had assured him, they would do all they could to prevent it, although they had many in their tribe who were too affectionate towards the English.

The same Indian also related that the Five Nations had begun to have some reflections, and feared that when they should no longer have the French, the English would wish to destroy them,[1] and that now they saw themselves encircled by their forts, and they could tell what would be their lot, by that which had happened to four nations who having asked for some powder, but got only a dozen pounds. The chiefs according to him were undecided, as to the course they should take, and the young men did not want to listen to them. They had also been notified by the Flat-Heads,[2] that the English wanted to destroy them, that they had made an incursion upon the English, and had killed a great number and taken several forts.[3] Finally they had returned to their cabins, where they were waiting for the news, and a decision

---

[1] They had cause to dread this, and made efforts to prevent it. Johnson alone was able to quiet them and make them forget their ancient political system in this war. Before this they were well convinced that they could not renounce it without the greatest danger. They appeared at all times to feel the necessity of putting France and England under obligation to seek them, and consequently to prevent one from prevailing against the other. On this principle they had in 1709, caused the loss of an English army destined to besiege Quebec, by corrupting the waters of a river near which they were encamped.— *Note in Original.*

[2] Cherokees and Catawbas.— *Ib.*

[3] This account was true as we have already spoken in a note.— *Ib.*

from the Five Nations, but that they had not replied to them.

On the 1st of July, M. Pouchot sent the prisoners with the news to Montreal. Several other Indians made similar reports. They described the uniforms of each regiment, and M. Pouchot knew, from having seen them, that they told the truth.

On the 3d of July, the son of Sonnonguires came to say to M. Pouchot, that he would return to his village, and hereafter remain quiet. His father pledged himself for his good behavior, and to prove this, he sent to M. Pouchot some certificates from the Ohio, which had been given him by a friend who was in the battle of Niagara, and who had taken them from some inhabitants of the Illinois to whom they belonged. He assured him that sooner than go to war against the French, he would go among the Flat Heads, the ancient enemies of his nation, and that when the English army was ready to leave, he would come to notify us.

On the 6th, there arrived a detachment and an officer whom M. Pouchot had sent to carry provisions to our vessels. They had been as far as to the bay of Corbeau, without finding them, because they had been cruising in the lake to observe what was passing at Oswego.

On the same day, the chiefs of La Presentation came to reply to M. Pouchot, by a very fine belt which he had sent them, to induce them to make a party to take some prisoners at Oswego. They begged him to be assured of their attachment, that they were very well contented to have him conduct their affairs, and that they never had a better father, but that this would be bringing a tomahawk upon the head of Kouatageté and his band. They exhorted M. Pouchot to have a little patience, until they could get some news from this chief, and said he had reason to be satisfied with them the more, as they were well encouraged and sustained by the nations below.

On the 13th, M. Pouchot sent a detachment to La Presentation,[1] which had been abandoned by the Indians of that mission since winter, to bring some planks and iron-work for the use of the fort, and to dismantle and ruin the missions so that they should not serve as a shelter for the enemy.

---

[1] The mission of La Presentation, was formed by the Abbé François Picquet, a Sulpician in 1749, for the settlement of emigrants from the Five Nations, chiefly Onondagas, who had been induced to settle under the protection of the French. This establishment was on the west side of the Oswegatchie, in the present village of Ogdensburgh. A store house and small fort were built, and the natural facilities of the country under the enterprise of the French soon rendered the colony prosperous and happy. After the conquest, the Oswegatchies remained near their former village, a considerable portion having removed to the north shore. Upon laying out the town of Johnstown, towards the close of the last century, they were removed to Indian Point in the town of Lisbon, some three miles below Ogdensburgh, and in 1806 the few that remained finally left for other parts. Some settled at St. Regis, and a few individuals returned to Onondaga. See *N. Y. Doc. Hist.*, i, 421; *Hist. St. Lawrence and Franklin Counties*.

La Gallette, on the north shore nearly opposite to La Presentation, had been proposed in 1708, as a favorable point for settlement, but the

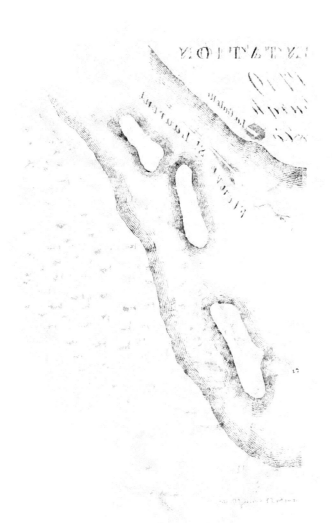

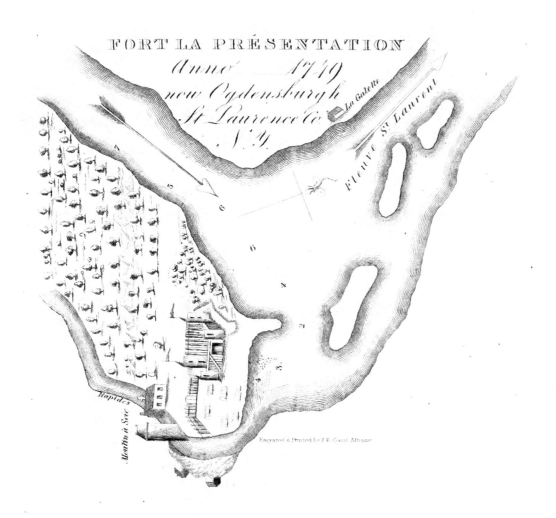

FORT LA PRÉSENTATION

Anno 1749

now Ogdensburgh

St Laurence Co

N 9

La Galette

Fleuve St Laurent

Rapides

Moulin à Scie

Engraved & Printed by J. E. Gavit Albany

About noon, an Indian of the Lake of Two Mountains arrived in three days from Oswego, and reported that Kouatageté and his band had been arrested by the English, and put under a strong guard, so that they should not lose sight of them, and that they had asked many times for their liberty, but always without avail. He informed us that the chiefs of the Five Nations who were at Oswego, had interceded for him, that they had held several councils at the quarters of the commandant on this subject, and that the son of Sonnonguires who had arrived, being strongly urged by the English said, that he had gone to Orakointon to strike his father, and that having seen him he had been so well received, and sent back without injury, and that they would do well to do the same.

This Indian related that they were daily expecting

suggestion remained over forty years unimproved. — *N. Y. Col. Hist.*, ix, 822.

The annexed engraving represents the place as seen in 1796. The site is adjacent to the depot of the Rome and Watertown Railroad. — ED.

2

the great English chief at Oswego,[1] where they had four
thousand men encamped. According to his description, there were there the Royal American, Gages, and
two battalions of the Royal Scotch, and some Rangers.
He added that they had formed a great camp at the
Falls, where they were making the portage of artillery,
and that the English army must amount to fifteen thousand men, under the great chief of all the English. Six
days after his arrival, Johnson would join with his
Indians, and then the whole army would set out. A
soldier had assured him, that they would start in about
ten days. This Indian had seen the artillery, of which
the English had mounted a hundred pieces. He had
distinguished twenty pieces cast of great calibre, of
which three were much larger than the rest. The
English had built five great bateaux, of thirteen oars
on each side, with a cannon at the end. He told us
that our vessel had appeared before the fort, and that
they had fired some cannon at it. The English then
sent against this vessel a large bateau which the French

---

[1] The British army under General Amherst, consisted of the first
and second battalion of Royal Highlanders (or 42d), 44th, 46th, 55th,
fourth battalion of the 60th, eight companies of the 77th, five of the
77th, five of the 80th, 597 grenadiers, 597 light infantry, 146 rangers,
three battalions of the New York regiment, the New Jersey regiment,
four battalions of the Connecticut regiment, and 167 of the Royal
Artillery. — *Mante*, 301.

The Rangers were under Captains Ogden and Waite; the New
Jersey troops under Col. Schuyler, those of New York under Colonels
Le Roux, Woodhull and Corsa, and those of Connecticut under Cols.
Lyman, Wooster, Fitch and Whiting. The artillery were under Col.
Williamson. — *Knox's Journal*, ii, 393. — ED.

allowed to approach, and then fired upon it when those in it returned. Finally they had sent parties to go to Niagara, where there had been an English vessel waiting for some time for some to come and take care of her.

M. Pouchot at once sent this Indian to carry this news down to the general. In the evening, M. Pouchot was notified of the arrival of the two French vessels at Toniata. On the 14th, La Force's canoe arrived, with letters, giving an account of his reconnoissance at Oswego, in which was a sketch of the position of the enemy very conformable to the account given by the Indian.

On the same day, at two o'clock in the afternoon, there came up a very violent storm from the northwest, with terrific thunder, and attended by a very singular phenomenon. This was a column of fire, which with a roar and lightning, fell upon the river near the end of the island. The waters rose so that they formed an immense wave, which after covering both ends of the island retired. It carried off a dock made for landing, sunk a Jacobite bateau, and filled the others, which were thrown upon the strand.[1]

On the 16th, M. Pouchot sent back the detachment which he had dispatched with provisions for the ves-

---

[1] Tornadoes have since repeatedly happened in this section of the country. Perhaps the most remarkable one on record occurred Sept. 20, 1845, beginning near Lake Ontario, and sweeping through the forest to Lake Champlain. — *Hist. of St. Lawrence and Franklin Counties*, p. 697. — ED.

sels, who soon returned, having executed their orders. La Force informed M. Pouilly, the lieutenant of the detachment, that from the quantity of barges that he had seen in the Oswego river, he thought this was the grand army, and from the fact that they had arrived in the interval between his two visits before Oswego, he judged they would be ready to leave in eight days. M. Pouchot sent these new observations to Montreal by an Indian.

On the 22d, a squaw of La Presentation, who had left two days before, said that there had arrived between sunset and ten o'clock in the evening, five Indians, an Onondaga and five [four?] Oneidas, all naked and armed with guns, pistols and tomahawks, had entered her cabin, and asked her many questions; namely, whether we had gone off from our island, if we had many people in the fort, if any had come from Montreal, and if we had many Indians. She answered them that we had many people in the fort, that they often arrived from Montreal, but that she did not know the number, and that the women did not meddle with such affairs. She said the French did not go out unless well guarded, and only worked on the islands near the fort. They asked if they were far off, and if they could not get upon the island to make a stroke. She replied that there was only one place in the fort where a landing could be made, and that this was always well guarded. They asked if he often sent people to Montreal. She replied that he often sent, but that they were always well escorted. They would not say where they were from, nor how long they had been out.

This woman asked of these Indians the news of Kouatageté and his people. They at first pretended not to know that they were at Oswego. She said to them, "It is then a long time since you set out." They replied "Kouatageté is safe; they will do him no harm, and you will soon see him back. He will come with all the English chiefs, and they will release him when the army moves." She told them that she and other women expected to go down to Montreal soon, because they were afraid. They assured her that they should not be harmed, but that they should only separate themselves from the French, which they invited them to do, and said they should keep themselves on the side of La Presentation and of Toniata, and then they would receive no injury. They pretended that they were stronger and more numerous than the English, and that they would come quickly, and in force from all the nations to prevent any harm from happening to the Indians.[1] They went off before day, and took away this woman's canoe. They told her that they would like to remain another day concealed, because if the French should come again to demolish the buildings they might find an opportunity to strike. She replied that they had made their last trip. Per-

---

[1] This was true. — *Note in Original.*

haps they did remain concealed through the day, but they did not dare to attack our detachment. The garrison had daily at least sixty men out working, and it is quite probable that the enemy might have succeeded in taking or killing some of them but for the precaution M. Pouchot had taken of getting the Indians to scatter through the neighborhood and watch for the enemy's parties. When the latter saw these scouts they returned, not seeking to do injury to their own people, and content with making war at the expense of the French or English only.

On the 24th, there arrived a convoy of provisions from Montreal. They announced that the English were above Richelieu, and that they feared the junction of Amherst with Murray, but they did not then know that there was so great an army on the side of St. Frederic. Meanwhile all these reports which M. Pouchot had obtained with so much care and diligence, gave very certain notions upon this subject.

On the 25th, at ten o'clock in the evening, the canoe of La Force arrived. By the letters which it brought we learned, that he observed the same camps at Oswego, and that on the 22d he had met near the Galloo Islands, an English vessel which was soon joined by another. Our corvette then took flight, and after having lost them both from view, came to anchor at Toniata.

On the 27th, seventy women, children and old

Indians left for Montreal, being driven off by fear.

On the 29th, at day break, the orators of La Presentation, called the "Chevalier de la Grimace," by the French, because he had a very wide mouth, and was a good speaker for an Indian, came to say to M. Pouchot, that some Missisakes living among them had said they saw in the direction of Cataracoui, ten bateaux full of English troops, with whom he had spoken.

At seven o'clock in the evening, there arrived eight canoes of Iroquois Indians, who had been driven by fear from their fishing at Toniata.[1] Among them was the Missisakes, whom he brought to be questioned. He related to M. Pouchot, that four days before, while fishing in the Bay of Cataracoui, he saw the two English vessels which were anchored near Little Cataracoui. He then took a fancy to see whether they had told him truely that the English would not hurt the Indians. He therefore went on board the great vessel, which had three decks, ten cannon on each side, a beam and some grapples. There were, according to him, a crew of one hundred men[2] upon each, half sailors and half soldiers, and a great many officers. The Missisake added that when he was at the Isle of Cedars, he saw ten bateaux pass laden with troops.

[1] A famous eel fishery. — *Note in Original.*
[2] There were 150. — *Ib.*

On the 30th, there arrived some more Indians from Toniata, who said they had heard the English pass in the night, at the Thousand Islands, a little below the Bay of Corbeau.

On the 1st of August, La Force sent his shallop to give notice that his vessel the *Iroquoise*, had struck upon a *poulier*,[1] in the middle of the river above Point au Baril. M. Pouchot at once sent some bateaux to aid in relieving her.

On the 5th, the vessels were anchored at La Presentation, and La Force came to the fort. This corvette made twelve inches of water an hour, and had fifteen feet of the forward part of her keel broken. They did all they could to repair her.

On the 8th, in the evening, Kouatageté arrived in three days from Oswego, with an Oneida and a Mohawk, as deputies sent by the Five Nations to engage our Indians to remain neutral. Kouatageté informed M. Pouchot that General Amherst had been fifteen days at Oswego, and that he had seen and spoken with him several times; that their army was about ten or fifteen thousand strong, consisting of eight regiments, a red with blue trimmings or red and yellow, a Scotch, a red with little black trimmings, Gage's regiment, light infantry. blue and red[2] and a great many with

---

[1] A mass of large pebbles, which form in the river like a rock.— *Note in Original.*

[2] The uniform of the Jersey Blues, was blue faced with scarlet. They were commanded by Schuyler, a brave and expert officer.— *Knox's Journal.*— ED.

caps,[1] and that he had counted sixty cannon. There had been left, according to his account, four large ones at the Falls where they had built a road by land to get them around. He said that the portage of the mortars had not yet been made, and he thought they could not be sent within ten days. He added, that he had met the vessels in the river, and that they were at work fortifying Oswego.

On the 10th, M. Pouchot was at the Isle Piquet, to assist in a council of the deputies of the Five Nations. They presented a very fine belt, not on behalf of Colonel Johnson, and upon which was represented the English, the Five Nations and the three villages of our Iroquois mission, Chouegatchi. The Lake and St. Louis,[2] with a man, and a fine road that led from one to the other, to invite our Indians to take it, and remain neutral, and let the whites fight and would soon make peace, and return the way they came without arms. They assured them that they would be well received, that Johnson and they had preceded the army only to see the whites fight. Johnson had told them that he only invited them for this purpose in 1755, 1758 and 1759, as they had been able to see the affairs of M. Dieskau and at Niagara, where without the Five Nations, the French had been beaten, without wishing to wait for better things. Another large belt from these nations expressed the same

---

[1] Militia.— *Note in Original.*

[2] Oswegatchi, Lake of Two mountains and Caughnawaga.— ED.

3

thing, and invited them to speak truly to them, that is to say, abide by their sentiments.

Then came some strings on behalf of General Amherst, to engage them to give attention to what these belts said, by which they assured them, that in five or six days, he would arrive at Chouegatchi, that he was coming to fight the French, and that the Master of Life alone knew what would happen.

The reply of our Indians was, to engage the deputies to go down to Montreal, and to the end of the road they had marked out, that as for them, they had no longer a fire kindled, since their father and the Iroquois of the Saut had agreed that the words that should come from the Five Nations should go directly to Montreal without stopping with them.

The deputies after having reflected much upon this answer which they were not expecting, replied that these words had been given them by the Five Nations at Oswego, and that they were sent here without having orders to proceed to Montreal, and that therefore they must return.

M. Pouchot, after having allowed them to finish their council, said to these Indians :— " If you chose to go down to Montreal I have nothing to say, and would let you speak with your father, but since you are going to return, I wish to say to you what I have in my heart. I do not give you formal words, and therefore they cannot listen to you. Only say from him whom you call The-midst-of-good-affairs, to your brothers the Iroquois, that their courage is lost, and that Johnson, with a little brandy, has made you follow him without wishing to look at the precipice towards which he is leading you. He makes all these warriors to march after him without having first consulted their chiefs, as you told me yourselves in 1755. He then wanted to go to Montreal to fight the French, and gave you supplies of merchandize. The fists of the French stopped him at Fort George. In 1758, the same thing happened. You reproached him, that a little troop of French had driven the English, and you returned ashamed of them. Did not I show you at Niagara, that you should not quit the hand of your father, if you wished to rest quietly upon your mats, and that they should be no longer stained with blood ? You listened to me then, and you retired to allow us to fight. Has Johnson heard these good things since your chiefs and those who came from the Ohio and wished to labor there in bringing peace to the land ? He is mocking you, because he is the stronger. If the great canoes of your father, the great Onontio, had not been taken, and if he had time to make others, rest assured that his children the French, would cover all this country like the trees. The English would soon be obliged to go and hide in a corner of the country,[1] where he would fly to the Abenakis. The French have only sought to have pity on his children,

---

[1] Acadia.— *Note in Original.*

and to furnish them their wants. They have never disturbed your mats, and your fires with their arms, to go and find the English in their country, from fear of killing you. You have never tried to stop them from passing, and now you are encircled by their forts, which they have asked of you to trap beavers. Where will you already go to seek the supply of your wants? See the condition of the Abenakis in their country! They go to the waters and the woods to get something to eat, and can no longer plant their Indian corn. They are the Englishmens' dogs, and they beat them with clubs or hang them when ever they please. The same thing will happen to you when the French are gone, and when you remind the English of their promises to supply your wants, they will mock at you, instead of its being as when you had the French and English for neighbors, and they gave to you out of jealousy of one another. Any Belts would have been useless to enable you to retain my advice, when you shall recall with the old people the good things which you have lost."

The deputies, although friends of the English, agreed that M. Pouchot had told the truth, and they confessed that they had not the courage of their ancestors. The Indians of Chouegatchi applauded this discourse very much. He made a present to the former, and sent them away.

On the 13th, five Indians brought letters from M. de Vaudreuil, to M. Pouchot. They informed that the English vessels were at Three Rivers, from St. Frederic and that the enemy were preparing to march. They were only waiting for Amherst on this side.

On the 15th, the *Iroquoise* was repaired. I ought here to relate an incident that deserves to be reported. Seventeen militia had deserted some days before, and one of them returned to the Cedars where he lived. His father, named Bray, a good old man, brought him back to his duty. He arrived this day and took his leave of him. The young man was unfortunately killed.

On the 16th, at seven o'clock in the evening, two Indians returning from the chase, announced that the English army was encamped at Point au Baril, and the advance-guard at La Presentation.[1] They had first gone on board the *Outaouaise*. La Broquerie, however, wrote nothing, but he fired three cannon. M. Pouchot sent two Frenchmen and two Indians in a canoe on board, to know what this meant. He sent word that the advance-guard of the enemy,[2] and the

---

[1] The English van-guard consisted of grenadiers, light infantry and rangers, under Colonel Francis Grant.— *Knox's Journal.*— ED.

[2] On the 5th of August, Sir William Johnson mustered 1,330 Indians, composed of the following tribes: Senesagos 329, Cayugas, 284, Tuscaroras 37, Canasaragas 20, Mohawks 51, Mohegans 12 Oquagos 18, Oswegatchies 15. The Belt Party 12, Senecas 114, Onondagas 203, Oneidas 60, Canajorakies 85, Schoharies 22, Chennogoas 31, Mawas 3, and Cannadroghas 34.

Notwithstanding this large number, when the army came to embark on the 14th, they were reduced to 706 in number.— *Knox's Journal*, ii, 403.— ED.

Indians in great numbers had landed at La Presentation, that he was observing them, and that the bulk
of the army had encamped at Point au Baril.

On the 17th, at three o'clock in the morning, M.
Pouchot dispatched a courier to M. de Vaudreuil, to
notify him of this event. At about seven o'clock, the
weather being very calm, General Amherst ordered
an attack upon the *Outaouaise*, which was in a place
where the currents could not be felt, — by six barges
called carcassieres, each carrying thirty men and a
twelve pounder. They surrounded this vessel, which
they first made to swing astern towards the north
bank, but a land battery obliged her to stand off.
After a cannonade of three hours upon both sides, she
was taken.[1]   M. Pouchot dispatched four shallops

---

[1] Mr. David Humphreys claims for Israel Putnam, then a lieutenant-colonel of Provincials in the English army, the merit of leading
the party that attacked and took this vessel. Although we place no
reliance upon this author as a historian, we will here give his account:
   " Two armed vessels obstructed the passage, and prevented the attack
on Oswegatchie. Putnam with one thousand men, in fifty bateaux,
undertook to board them. This dauntless officer, ever sparing of the
blood of others, as prodigal of his own, to accomplish it with the
least loss, put himself (with a chosen crew, a beetle and wedges), in
the van, with a design to wedge the rudders, so that the vessels should
not be able to turn their broadsides, or perform any other manœuvre.
All the men in his fleet were ordered to strip to their waistcoats and
advance at the same time. He promised if he lived, to join and show
them the way up the sides. Animated by so daring an example, they
moved swiftly, in profound stillness, as to certain victory or death.
The people on board the ships, beholding the good countenance with
which they approached, ran one of the vessels on shore, and struck
the colors of the other. Had it not been for the dastardly conduct of
the ship's company in the latter, who compelled the captain to haul

with some swivels to the orders of La Force, captain of the *Iroquoise*, but this vessel had surrendered before they could join her.[1] M. Pouchot had hoped that the *Outaouaise* would have approached and put herself

down his ensign, he would have given the assailants a bloody reception; for the vessels were well provided with spars, nettings, and every customary instrument of annoyance as well as defence."

This poetical historian has given an account of the subsequent capture of the fort, which, if deviation from facts, be regarded as a measure of merit, deserves the highest rank among works of fiction. He says:

" It now remained to attack the fortress, which stood on an island, and seemed to have been rendered inaccessible by an high abattis of black ash, that everywhere projected over the water. Lieutenant-Colonel Putnam proposed a mode of attack, and offered his services to carry it into effect. The general approved the proposal. Our partisan, accordingly, caused a sufficient number of boats to be fitted for the enterprise. The sides of each boat were surrounded with fascines, musket proof, which covered the men completely. A wide plank, twenty feet in length, was then fitted to each boat in such a manner, by having an angular piece sawed from one extremity, that when fastened by ropes on both sides of the bow, it might be raised or lowered at pleasure. The design was, that the plank should be held erect, while the oarsmen forced the bow with the utmost exertion against the abattis; and that afterwards being dropped on the pointed brush, it would serve them as a kind of bridge, to assist them in passing over them. Lieutenant-Colonel Putnam having made his dispositions to attempt the escalade in many places at the same moment, advanced with his boats in admirable order. The garrison perceiving these extraordinary and unexpected machines, waited not the assault, but capitulated. Lieutenant-Colonel Putnam was particularly honored by General Amherst, for his ingenuity in this invention, and promptitude in its execution. — *Humphrey's Writings*, p. 280.

It is unfortunate for the permanent fame of General Putnam, that it depends upon such authority. — ED.

[1] The account given by KNOX, ii, p. 404, is as follows:

" 17th. The Outawa brig attempted to escape up the river very early in the morning, but was intercepted by our row gallies commanded by Colonel Williamson, who attacked her vigorously, when after an obstinate engagement of two hours and upwards, wherein she had

under the protection of the fort, which she could have done had she been able to place herself at the head of the currents.

On the 18th, the enemy left La Presentation with a

---

fifteen men killed and wounded, her commander, M. de la Broquerie, thought proper to strike. It has been observed before, that four of these galleys carried each a brass twelve pounder, and the fifth a howitzer. This is a remarkable action, and does great credit to the colonel, who was a volunteer on the occasion ; for the brig mounted one eighteen pounder, seven twelve pounders, two eights, with four swivels, and had one hundred men on board, being a top sail, of near one hundred and sixty tons. She discharged seventy-two rounds, and the gallies, who had five officers and twenty-five artillerymen only exclusive of provincial rowers, fired one hundred and eighteen.

The general was highly pleased at this capture, which he testified by his acknowledgments to the colonel and officers, with a generous reward to the gunners. Such was the service performed by four guns and one howitzer, with the sole loss of one man killed and two wounded."

An account quoted by Knox (ii, 409), says, that the action lasted two hours and a quarter, and that the howitzer only fired twice as some timbers in that galley gave way. It further adds : "On board of the galleys, independent of the provincials who only rowed, were twenty-five of the Royal Artillery, together with Captain Starkey, Lieuts. Williamson, Standish, Davis and Conner, six to each vessel, and Colonel Williamson rowed in a small boat from galley to galley, giving directions how to attack most effectually and with greatest safety." The general gave the artillerymen twenty-five guineas.

The affair is related by Mante as follows :

"On the 17th, the row galleys well manned, advanced with the utmost intrepidity, under a very heavy fire from the enemy, but it did not in the least damp the ardor of the assailants. Their fire was returned with such resolution and bravery, that after a severe contest of about four hours, the French vessel struck her colors. She mounted ten twelve pounders, and had on board one hundred men, twelve of whom were killed or wounded. Two of Col. Williamson's detachment were killed and three wounded. The general immediately named the vessel the Williamson, in honor of the colonel, and to perpetuate the memory of so gallant an action." — ED.

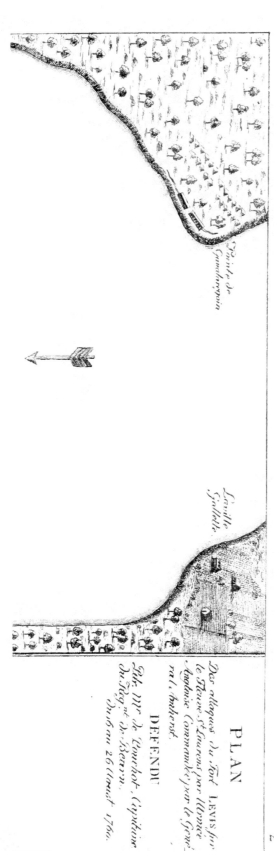

PLAN

Des attaques du Fort LEVIS sur
le Fleuve St Laurent par l'armée
Angloise Commandée par le Gené-
ral Amherst.

DÉFENDU

Par Mr de Pouchot, Capitaine
du Reg.t de Berry.
Du 6 au 26 Aoust 1760.

Pointe de
Ganatherapoin

Laville
Gallotte

2

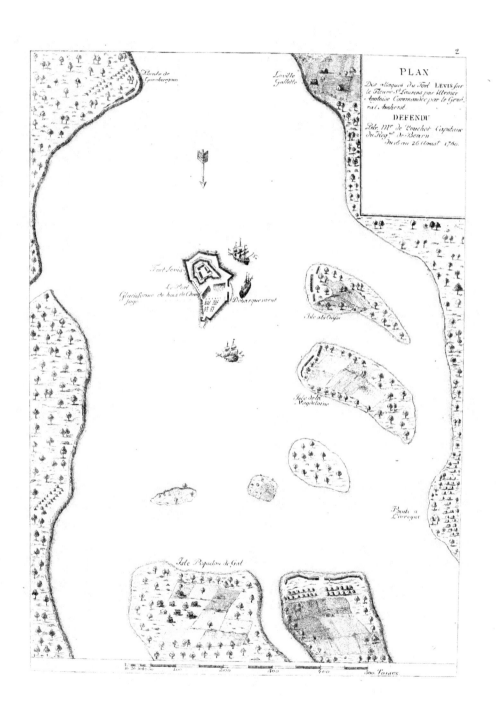

PLAN
Des attaques du Fort LEVIS sur
le Fleuve St Laurens par l'Armée
Angloise Commandée par le Géné-
ral Amherst.

DEFENDU
Pdr Mr de Pouchot Capitaine
du Régt de Bearn
Pris le au 26 Aoust 1760.

Pointe de
Ganatarepin

La ville
Gallette

Fort Levis
Le Port
Glacissforme de bois de Chesne
juge
Debarquement

Isle a la Cuisse

Isle de la
Magdelaine

Pointe a
L'iroquse

Isle Piquelon le Gal

fresh breeze. Their whole army remained about four hours in battle array in their bateaux at the beginning of the rapids, forming a very fine spectacle. M. Pouchot then thought that they intended to attack with a strong force, and make an entry upon the Island. He had accordingly so placed nine cannon to fight up the river and had placed the others in the epaulment, so that they could make eleven rebounds upon the water. It is thought that the enemy would have lost heavily before they could have secured a landing, if they had entertained such a thought. They determined to file a'ong the north shore with a considerable interval between one bateau and another, to escape the fire of artillery from the fort. They caused the *Outaouaise* which they had taken, to approach to within half cannon shot to cover them.[1]

M. Pouchot only sought to retard their passage by four pieces which he could bring to bear upon them. We fired a hundred and fifty cannon shot with very little damage, which appeared to us to be occasioned by the wind being strong, and the currents made them quickly loose the point of aim. As M. Pouchot knew many of the officers of this army, several of them bade him good day in passing: and others thought from our allowing them to pass that they were his friends, but did not stop to pay any compliments. The

---

[1] Under Lieut. Sinclair. — *Knox.*— ED.

[2] Under General Amherst in person.— *Ib.*— ED.

4

greater part of the army encamped at Point d' Ivrogne. They also threw quite a force upon La Cuisse, la Magdelaine and Les Galots Islands.

On the 19th, their regiment of artillery left Old Gallette, with all their field artillery, and defiled past as the former had done, to go and encamp at Point d' Ivrogne. The vessel kept up the heaviest fire possible to cover them. We fired but little at the bateaux, because it was attended with but little success, but rather directed our attention to the vessel. Of fifty shots that we fired, at least forty-eight went through the body of the vessel, which obliged them to get a little further away. Their captain named Smul, behaved with the greatest bravery, walking continually on the deck in his shirt sleeves. He had many men disabled.

The two other vessels, one of twenty-two cannon, eights and sixes, named the *Seneca*, and the other of eighteen pieces of sixes, named the *Oneida*,[1] came in the evening, and took position by the side of the former.

On the 20th, there was quite a movement of the enemy's army, and a great number of bateaux went

---

[1] These vessels were named by Knox, the *Onondaga* (Capt. Loving), and the *Mohawk* (Lieut. Phipps). The *Iroquoise*, is not subsequently mentioned. She was probably so disabled as to be incapable of service in the actions.

The French are said to have had five small row galleys but made no use of them. According to Mante, the English had twenty-one killed, and nineteen wounded.— ED.

and came from their camp at La Presentation. They also encamped two regiments at Point de Ganataragoin, who began to throw up earth works on that side, as also on the island La Cuisse and la Magdelaine. We fired some volleys of cannon at them to disturb the laborers, but had to be extremely saving in our powder, not having more than five thousand pounds when the enemy arrived.

On the 21st, every thing remained quiet, as the enemy were working with their full force on their batteries. Their vessels withdrew also beyond cannon range. We fired on the laborers, but without much result, as they were already covered, and their ground was some twenty-four feet higher than that of the island.

By noon we discovered their embrasures, and in the evening their bateaux made a general movement, and we counted as many as thirty-six barges carrying each at least twenty men, who threw themselves into the three vessels, from which we judged that they were going to attack the next morning. We consequently worked to make epaulments of wood to cover the parties that we thought would be the most exposed in the direction of the enemy's batteries. All the artillery was loaded with shot and grape, and every one was ordered to pass the night at his post.

On the 22d, at five in the morning, the three vessels approached to within about two hundred toises of the fort, and occupied the whole range of the river above,

from the Island La Cuisse to Point Ganataragoin,
from which we thought they intended to cannonade
us vigorously from the vessels and land batteries.
They formed together a half circle around the fort.
Consequently M. Pouchot ordered the artillery officer
to collect his pieces of artillery, and put them under
cover of merlons, so that they should not be dismounted. He also masked his embrasures with the
ends of great logs of wood to represent cannon. We
were only clear and in condition to resist from above.

As soon as the vessels were placed, they began a
very brisk and continuous fire, from twenty-five cannon and at the same time the enemy unmasked the
battery at Ganataragoin, consisting of two twenty-
fours, and four twelves, as also that on the Island of
La Cuisse, of fourteen pieces of twelves and eighteens,
and a third one on the Isle la Magdelaine, of two
pieces of twenty-four, and six of twelve. At the first
volley M. Bertrand, artillery officer, was instantly
killed by a cannon ball through his loins, as he stood
pointing out to M. Pouchot the calibre of their guns.

A quarter of an hour later, they began to throw
bombs from the Island la Magdelaine, where they had
two twelve-inch bomb mortars, six mortars for royal
grenades, and two howitzers. On the Island La
Cuisse six mortars for royal grenades, and on Point
Ganataragoin two twelve inch mortars, two for royal
grenades and two howitzers, making in all seventy-
five mouths of fire.

M. Pouchot received quite a bruise from a piece of wood ten feet long, and fourteen inches square which a twelve inch bomb knocked over, injuring his back, but this did not prevent him from being wherever he was needed.

All these batteries were served with the greatest vigor and without ceasing till noon, and made the fort fly into pieces and splinters. Our men remained under cover, each one at his post, and the sentinels only observed the movements of the enemy. Thinking from our silence that we were perhaps disconcerted, they advanced their vessels to within pistol shot of the fort. They were filled with troops, even to the rigging, and were supported by the fire of all the land batteries.

Fortunately they could only come before the fort one by one, from the manner in which the first vessel came up, and which saw as far to the entrance of the fort, which was also enfiladed by the battery of La Magdelaine. M. Pouchot had in advance covered this with heavy blindages, leaving only a passage sufficient for one man.

He thought that the enemy intended to attack with a heavy force. At least three thousand men, volunteers, grenadiers and light troops, were embarked in bateaux, and placed behind the point of La Cuisse Island, from whence they could emerge under the aid of the fire of the three vessels and the land batteries.

The movements of the vessels soon induced M.

Pouchot to place 150 men, and four officers on the side opposite the epaulment. He fought the vessels one after another with five guns, the only ones that were mounted, charged with balls and grape, without replying to the land batteries.

Notwithstanding the superiority of the enemy's fire with our five pieces and our musketry, we forced the *Outaouaise* and then the *Oneida*, to run aground half a league from the fort, near the Galot Islands. One of the two was not in further condition to serve. The *Seneca* of 22 guns, in trying to come nearer the fort grounded also, and was so cut to pieces that she struck her flag, having then on board three hundred and fifty men. The side of the vessel towards the fort was in very bad condition, her battery touched the water and her port holes made only one opening. The water she had taken in made her lean towards the fort.[1] M. Pouchot gave orders to discontinue the

---

[1] " The *Mohawk* came down without the other two, who seemed inclinable to follow, and fired briskly, when very near the fort, for a considerable time, but was so roughly handled that she was obliged to cut her cable and away, for fear of sinking. By this time the *Williamson* came into play, but receiving a shot at an unlucky place, started a plank, which obliged her to retire to a neighboring island to be repaired. The *Onondaga* at length came down, but not taking the same course, stopped in shallow water pretty near the enemy, who fired every time into her, when she could not help herself. Though within four hundred yards of one of our batteries, she struck to the enemy, and sent a bateau to them with four men, and Mr. Thornton, the commodore's second, who looking at that distance so like Loring, they thought at the batteries it was he. The same boat rowing back again to the ship, with one of her crew, probably to fire her, Capt. Adam Williamson, the engineer, pointed a gun and

fire as he wished to save his powder. The second captain, and some sailors came to surrender. M. Pouchot retained them as hostages, but could not receive the whole, as they were more numerous than his garrison.

In the intervals between these combats, the enemy attempted to land two or three times, to make an attack from the point opposite the Isle la Caisse. Two guns that were pointed in that direction restrained them, and made them retire behind that point. It is probable that the bad condition in which they found their vessels, took away their desire of advancing. This action lasted from five in the morning, to half past seven in the evening, without the fire ceasing. We had forty men killed or wounded. We cannot too much praise the firmness which the officers, colonial soldiers, militia and especially the cannoniers, who were sailors, displayed on the oc-

---

fired through her, taking both that fellow's arms off, which made her row into shore directly. Perceiving then there was a squabble on board the *Onondaga*, about what they should do, the general sent an officer's party on board [Lieutenant Pennington,] who hoisted the colors again and saved her for ourselves."— *Account quoted by Knox.*

The General ordered Lieut. Sinclair from the *Williamson* Brig, and Lieut. Pennington, with two detachments of grenadiers under their command to take possession of the *Onondaga*, " and they obeyed their orders with such undaunted resolution that the English colors were again hoisted on board her. But the vessel after all, could not be got off; and was therefore abandoned about midnight. The English batteries, however, put a stop to any attempt of the enemy to board her. Capt. Loring being wounded, was in the mean time sent ashore."— *Mante.*— ED.

casion. Three or four of the latter could never be rewarded for their address and activity in serving their pieces. The enemy, like ourselves, fired ball and grape constantly. M. Pouchot directed a blacksmith to cut up some old irons with which he filled sacks and put into the bore of his guns, adding a ball, which did terrible execution upon the vessels, on account of the height of the ramparts which placed them under our fire, so that we could see upon their decks.

One thing which amused the garrison at the most serious moments of the battle was, that the Indians, who were perched upon their trenches and batteries, to watch the contest with the vessels, which they regarded as on their side, on account of the names that had been given them, and because they carried an Indian painted upon their flags,— made furious cries at seeing them so mal-treated. The English had assured them that with these vessels alone, they would make the place surrender. When these Indians saw them drift off and ground, they redoubled their cries, and sung out railing names at the English, saying: — "You did not want to kill our father at Niagara : see how you are taking him! If you had listened to us, you would not have been here! A Frenchman's fist has made you cringe!" This action had, however, dismantled all the tops of the parapets around half of the fort, thrown down the fascines that were placed on the side of La Cuisse Island, and in front of the two demi-bastions.

At night, M. Pouchot endeavored to repair with sacks of earth, the batteries of the bastion opposite the island so that they could be served. This bastion was ready to tumble down, and we could have walked upon the slope formed by the earth that had fallen down.

The enemy continued through the night to bombard us, and fired volleys of cannon from each battery, loaded with shot and grape, at intervals, to prevent us from making repairs. We had two men killed and several wounded.

On the 23d, the enemy continued to bombard and cannonade vigorously all day. At night we tried the same bombardment and volleys of cannon at intervals as on the night previous.

On the 24th, they unmasked a new battery to break down the wooden redoubt at the end of the island, and to enfilade our intrenchments on the side opposite the islands. Their batteries continued as violently as on the preceding days, and fires caught in the ruins of the magazine, and in the quarters of the commandant, but these were happily extinguished without the enemy observing our difficulty. We had but little trouble to take care of what little powder and balls we had left. The enemy's batteries dismounted all the cannon of the bastion opposite the islands. The coffers of the parapets were razed down to within two feet of the terre plein, greatly exposing the powder magazine, which was only made of some large beams.

5

On the 25th, at day break, M. Pouchot fired vigorously three pieces upon the batteries which troubled us the most, and which were the only ones left on the side attacked. Even one of these three pieces and the most important one, wanted a third of its length, having broken twice. Notwithstanding its calibre, we put in two or three small balls. We had perceived by the enemy's movements, that this kind of firing troubled them much in their trenches, but we found it out of our power to ruin or even to materially injure their batteries.

The activity of our fire put the English in bad humor, and in the afternoon they redoubled theirs from all their batteries, and fired red-hot balls, fire-pots and carcases. This was too much for this miserable fort, which was now only a litter of carpenter's wood and fascines. The hot shot set fire to the saucissons of the interior revetment of the bastion, already down, but we extinguished it. From this we may see how the rampart was ruined. Some fire-pots also kindled twice in the debris of the fort, and we also extinguished these flames with water found in the holes made by bursting bombs.

This determined M. Pouchot, with the advice of all the officers of the garrison, to write to General Amherst, complaining against this kind of warfare never used but against rebels, and which should not be practiced against a brave garrison which deserved not such treatment. In reply he sent his aid-de-camp with a kind of capitulation for us to surrender as prisoners of war, with the threat that if we did not accept within half an hour, he would resume hostilities.

M. Pouchot received the officer, and read what Amherst demanded before all the officers and the garrison. The latter made the most urgent entreaties for him to accept them, in view of the impossibility of escaping a general conflagration in case of a fire, on account of the small capacity of the fort and the incumbrance of the ruins.

There remained at this time on the front attacked, only two cannon in condition to fire, and no more balls. The outer batteries of the fort were all ruined, as they were commanded by the islands, as were also the epaulments of the intrenchments, which were no cover against an assault.

On the 26th, in the morning, when the enemy entered,[1] they were greatly surprised at seeing only a

[1] 18th August. The weather is extremely unfavorable to our operations, yet the general intent on the vigorous prosecution of his measures resolves to lose no time; this morning was taken up with the repairs of the row galleys and prize vessel, and at ten o'clock the engineers with the covering party returned, and made their report; but his Excellency was predetermined, and the army are in readiness. The first division, consisting of the grenadiers, two battalions of light infantry, the right brigade of regulars, Schuyler's regiment, the greatest part of the Indians with Sir William Johnson, three row galleys and some field artillery, are to proceed down by the north shore, commanded by the general in person; pass the fort and take possession of the islands and coasts below it. At the same time the second division, composed of the left brigade of regulars, Lyman's regiment, two ranging companies, the remainder of the Indians, and two row galleys, under the command of Colonel Haldimand, to row

few soldiers scattered around their posts which they left,
and some sixty militia, with handkerchiefs on their
heads, in their shirt sleeves, and with necks bare as is
the Canadian fashion. They asked M. Pouchot where
was his garrison? He replied that they saw the whole.
We had more than sixty men killed or wounded. All
the officers had been more or less wounded.

down to the south coast, and take post opposite to the fort, where
they will not be exposed to the fire of the place, whilst the prize now
deservedly called the *Williamson* brig, under Lieutenant Sinclair, will
sail down the centre of the river, between the two divisions with
directions to moor at random shot from the fort; Brigadier Gage, with
the rest of the army and heavy artillery, to remain at Oswegatchie.
Such is the disposition his Excellency made before the return of the
engineers, and it was spiritedly executed accordingly, under a brisk
and continued cannonade, directed against the brig and the general's
column, whereby one galley was sunk, ten men were killed and
wounded, one of whom lost a thigh, and many bateaux and oars
were grazed with shot; as the north division rowed down in single
files it was eleven at night before the sternmost boat joined, and
then the blockade of the fort was completely formed. Our Indians
landed on the islands Gallop and Picquet, which the enemy abandoned with great precipitation, having left a number of scalps, two
swivel guns, some barrels of pitch, a quantity of tools and utensils,
with some iron behind them; our Indians were so exasperated at
finding the scalps, that they fired all their houses, not sparing even
the chapel.

Late in the night an attempt was made to weigh up the galley that
was sunk, but we could not succeed.

19*th*. The General with Colonel Williamson and Lieutenant-Colonel
Eyre, reconnoitred the fort and the islands nearest to it, on two of
which ground is made choice of for batteries, about six hundred yards
from the fort, as also for a third on an advantageous point of land on
the south shore, and detachments are immediately ordered to break
ground, cut and make fascines with every other preparation for carrying on the siege. Orders were sent to Oswegatchie for the heavy
artillery, which are expected down this night. The *Onondaga* and
Mohawk appeared to-day; they received orders in like manner as

The enemy admitted that in their passage to encamp, a carcassiere had sunk, and that six bateaux were shot through, of which that of General Amherst was one. He had been watching most attentively.   This general politely reproached M. Pouchot, who answered : " Sir, we only wanted to pay you the honors to which you are entitled.".

---

the brig to come to anchor at random shot from the fort, and if cannonaded not to return it. The remainder of the army except one Connecticut regiment, are ordered down from Oswegatchie, whence our heavy artillery arrived late at night, and the row galley with her gun were weighed up.

The fort fired on the brig yesterday which she spiritedly returned until ordered to desist.

22*d*. The troops have worked with such diligence that our batteries will be completed this night, and ready to play on Fort Lévis tomorrow.

23*d*. The batteries were opened this morning, and had such effect that the enemy drew in their guns and endeavored to serve them *à couverte*. After some hours firing, a disposition was made to storm the fort with the grenadiers of the army, in which the three vessels were to have assisted ; for this purpose a number of marksmen were judiciously placed on board each ship, with the view of compelling the enemy to abandon their guns ; and they were ordered to fall down on the fort, within the range of small arms ; but whether the vessels were confused with the weight of the enemy's fire, or that the miscarriage may be imputed to the navigation or the wind, is difficult to determine, for the general, not approving of their manner of working down, sent orders to them to return to their former station and desisted from his project for the present. The garrison expended a great deal of ammunition to a little purpose ; and our artillery were so well served that the enemy were rather shy of standing to their guns.

25*th*. We have had warm cannonading on both sides, but their guns being at length dismounted by our superior fire, M. Pouchot, the governor, after displaying as much gallantry as could be expected in his situation, beat a *chamade*, and in the afternoon capitulated for his garrison, who are become prisoners of war ; they consist of two cap-

The English had one hundred and twenty-eight men killed or wounded upon the *Oneida*, which was grounded. Upon the *Mohawk*, the captain was wounded and fifty men disabled. Upon the *Outaouaise*, which they had taken from us, fifty-four men, and on the different occasions in which they had approached the fort a hundred. To this should be added what they lost in

---

tains, six subalterns and two hundred and ninety-one men, all ranks included; they had a lieutenant of artillery with twelve men killed, and thirty-five wounded. The ordnance mounted at Fort Lévis are twelve twelve pounders, two sixes, thirteen fours, four of one pound each, and four brass six pounders. Lieutenant-Colonel Massey has taken possession of the fort with three companies of his battalion. Fort Lévis, on the Isle Royale, is a most advantageous situation; the island is small, and entirely comprehended within the works, which are carried on in the same irregular manner as nature has formed the insulary shores about it, but the area of the fort is a regular square within four bastions only, which seems to have been the first intention in fortifying the island, so that the other defences to all appearance have been occasionally added to render the place more respectable, and cut off our communication to Montreal, to which it was an excellent barrier, at the head of a number of dreadful rapids, and commands in a great measure the navigation between Lake Ontario and Canada. The country north and south, is apparently even, rich, and capable of great improvement, inhabited principally by Indians, which, with the uncommon fertility of the circumjacent islands, producing Indian and other corn in great abundance, and the prospect of an immense fur trade, induced the governor general to establish a strong settlement in this district. The batteries erected against Fort Lévis consisted of six guns each, besides mortars, though designed for a greater number if necessary, and the two islands whereon they are constructed are occupied chiefly by Col. Massey's grenadiers, with Brigadier Gage's and Colonel Amherst's corps of light infantry, who first took possession of them; and the remainder of the army except Col. Haldimand's detachment, on the fourth point battery are dispersed on the other contiguous islands in such a manner as to surround the fortress and cut off the enemy's retreat, in case they had been inclined to abandon and retire." — *Knox's Journal*, ii, 405.

their batteries and trenches, and which they never would confess.[1]

The surrender of the fort being made, several colonels came to conduct M. Pouchot to General Amherst. They showed him a thousand attentions. He had seen some of them at Niagara and at New York. They feared that the Indians who were very threatening, and who were disappointed in finding nothing in the fort which the soldiers had pillaged, might wish to do some harm. He thanked them for their attentions.[2]

Having landed on the shore, many Indians came to see M. Pouchot, who recognized several of their chiefs. He said to them: "You have killed your father; if they are not people of courage so much the worse for

[1] On the capitulation of Fort Levi, the Indians, having found in the deserted cabins of the enemy a few Mohawk scalps, wished at once to fall upon the garrison and commence a general massacre. Sir William's influence, however, again prevailed, and, though not without much ill temper, they retired to their encampment. That same night, while the savages, deeply chagrined, were brooding over this fancied grievance, an officer, partly in anger and partly in jest, observed to some one in his tent, that the English would, on their return from the expedition, exterminate the Indian race. An Indian, overhearing the remark, communicated it to his companions, seven hundred of whom immediately loaded their muskets, and in great wrath threatened to return home, declaring that it was high time to provide for the security of their families. The next day many of them made good their threats, "though there still remained a sufficient number," wrote Johnson to Secretary Pitt, "to answer our purpose and bring us constant intelligence." — *Stone's Life of Sir William Johnson*, ii, 129. — ED.

[2] The English changed the name of the fort to *Fort William Augustus*, and left a garrison of two hundred men under Captain Osborne, and also the sick and wounded a hundred and fifty in number. The army left on the 31st. — ED.

you." They replied: "Don't be disheartened, father; you will go to the other side of the great lake, we will soon rid ourselves of the English." They were surprised to see him so tranquil.

General Amherst held a conversation for an hour with M. Pouchot in private. He wished information as to what remained to be done in the campaign. It may be presumed that the latter did not make him think he had an easy task. He, in common with the whole army, appeared especially to dread the passage of the rapids.[1] They took among the Canadians thirty-six guides for their bateaux. The garrison and officers were conducted by way of Oswego to New York. M. Belle-Garde, Sulpician missionary at La Presentation, who had chosen to be shut up in the fort to serve the wounded, obtained leave to go down to Montreal with two or three women. This priest was very worthy on account of his zeal for religion, which had led him to Canada for the sole purpose of converting the Indians. The English sent him back to his mission.[2] The English army remained about fifteen days, making arrangements to go down the river, but notwithstanding their guides, of whom perhaps some

[1] In this passage the English lost forty-six bateaux, seventeen whaleboats, one row galley, and eighty-four men. — ED.

[2] There were two priests named La Garde in Canada at this time. Jean Pierre Besson de La Garde arrived in 1750, and died April 11, 1790. Pierre Paul Frs de La Garde arrived in 1755, and died at Montreal, April 4, 1784.—*Liste Chronologique.* The latter was with Pouchot at the time of the siege.— ED.

sought the worst channels, they lost eighty bateaux and their carcassiers at Coteau lu Lue.

The Chevalier de la Corne, who was watching the English, with a body of militia at the head of the Cedars, having learned of their arrival fell back step by step to the Island of Montreal. The enemy landed at a quarter of a league above that place, and sent deputies at once to agree upon the capitulation which is known to the world. All the troops and Canadian officers who wished to leave the country,[1] were sent to France in English vessels, upon condition of not again serving in the war.

We may well suppose, that during the course of this wretched campaign, every thing went up to an excessive price.[2] The intendant caused certificates to

---

[1] They were urgently solicited by the English to decide upon this, as they wished to get rid of as many of them as possible.— *Note in Original.*

There were sent to France, about 185 officers, 2,400 artillerists, and land or colonial troops, including sick and wounded, and somewhat over 500 sailors, domestics, women and children. The remaining five or six hundred soldiers married in Canada, took land, and abandoned their flag, to remain in America.— *Garneau,* iii, 272.

The total effective force of Canada, including militia, at the time of the surrender was 20,433.— *Knox,* ii, 441.— ED.

[2] M. Bertyer, minister of Marine, had determined to send some provisions, but their price, with high freights, delayed day after day, the departure of the transport vessels, which were finally unable to enter the river St. Lawrence, and were burned in the bay of Chaleurs. The Marquis de Vaudreuil had foreseen this want of succor, and had ordered Sieur de Minville to cruise with his frigate at the mouth of the river. Fourteen English ships laden with munitions for Quebec were taken, but he was obliged to burn them without being able to derive any advantage from them.— *Note in Original.*

serve for all the extraordinary expenses occasioned by the scarcity and high price of all the provisions, but he would not convert them into bills of exchange, except for those whom he favored, so as not to surprise France at these enormous expenses. There remained in the hands of the inhabitants and other individuals, an enormous quantity of orders and certificates, which he would not convert into bills of exchange.

The English being masters of Canada, felt their advantage over the French in collecting these at an early moment, as we may well believe, and to solicit for their payment, which they obtained.[1] It is no exaggeration to say, that the sums which France was forced to pay under this agreement, would amount to from twenty-three to twenty-six millions. If the fear of paying this entered into the consideration of ceding Canada they were mistaken.

M. Pouchot and all the French officers with the French and Colonial soldiers were by virtue of the capitulation of Montreal, to be sent to France, and the Canadians to their own country. The former departed from New York on the first of January, and after a very stormy passage arrived at the roadstead of

---

[1] By a special declaration signed at Paris, on the 10th of February 1763, the king agreed to pay the bills of exchange and the certificates which had been given to the Canadians for supplying the French troops, by a liquidation that should cease within a convenient time, according to distance and difficulties of rendering.— *Note in Original.*

Spithead, where they remained fifteen days and finally landed at Havre de Grace on the 8th of March, 1761.

In this passage, they witnessed three very curious phenomena. The first, was that in a very great storm, the sea sparkled on the tops of all the waves like lightning in a dark night. The second, was a rainbow whose two ends reached from larboard to starboard, across the stern of the vessel, and followed its wake like a cord drawn after it. The third, was a fine lunar rainbow, well formed, but with colors less bright than a solar one, and the moon was at the same time quite yellow.

FRAGMENT UPON THE FRENCH COLONY
OF CANADA.

———————

Canada was at first settled by fishermen; by individuals who came to trade with the Indians,— by discharged soldiers, and finally by people who had been sent thither from France, under *lettres de cachet*. Some of these latter, were for three years before they could recover their liberty, and others were for life. Some others, if not the greater number, had been sent out by the Seigneurs of the country to establish themselves.

The lands had been at first ceded by the king to the foreign missions, the Sulpicians, the Jesuits and to officers. There were found in Canada few lands, and perhaps none, that belonged to the merchants or peasantry.

That which still further contributed to the increase of these establishments was, the discharge of the Regiment of Carignan, of which all the soldiers became colonists, and the officers, proprietors of the lands belonging to the laity.[1] Such were the actual

———————

[1] This occurred about a century previous to the time the above was written.— ED.

sources of population of this immense country. It appears strange, from the little care and aid given to increase it, that this colony, which was so long very feeble, and often ready to perish with misery from the little help it got from France, should notwithstanding this, have gained a population of thirty thousand souls.[1] From this we may infer that the climate is fine and the soil fertile. It is not unusual to find from grandfather to grandchildren, as many as sixty persons.

The Canadians are very well formed, robust, and active, endure pain and fatigue admirably, and are accustomed to long and painful journeys for their trade, which they accomplish with great address and patience. These voyages are usually made very deliberately, on account of the kind of life which they lead on these occasions. They are brave, love war, and are ardent patriots. They evince a strong attachment to their mother country, and their little knowledge of the world renders them volunteer braggarts and liars, being little informed upon any subject.

There is no country where women lead a happier life than in Canada. The men show them great at-

---

[1] This is a great error. By a census taken about the middle of the century, it appears that the colony of Canada then had about 88,000 souls. The last enumeration, under Governor Carlton, brought up the population to 153,000, of which 3,000 were English and protestants, who had settled there since the peace. The latter held all the commerce in their hands, and sought to make themselves sole masters of the administration.— *Note in Original.*

tentions, and spare them all the fatigue they can.   We
might also add, that they deserve all this, being mod-
est, of comely figure, vivacious in spirit, and full of
intrigue.   It is only through them, that their husbands procure employment that puts them at ease
and above the common lot.   There prevails in the
villages, a tone of good society which we would not
expect in a country so remote.   They dance and demean
themselves very gracefully, and this without masters.

The Canadians are generally religious and of good
morals.   The voyageurs are but little trusty in the
affairs of trade.   Their priests restrain them severely,
being their temporal and spiritual masters, and have
brought all under their sway, even to the general and
intendant, for it would be a misfortune for the two
latter not to secure their good will.   The curates are
rich and removable.   The bishop of the greatest diocese in the world,— that of Quebec, has rents of sixteen thousand livres, and is responsible only to the
pope.   Since the death of M. de Pombriant, the English have not nominated one, and the whole country
is under the direction of two grand vicars.[1]

---

[1] The famous bill of 1774, allowed the Canadian catholics to have a
bishop, but upon condition that he should not be consecrated in
France.   They raised all manner of clamors and troubles from one
cause and another in England, upon the promulgation of this
bill.   This justifies the reflections of the author of *Observations sur
le traité de paix conclu à Paris en 1763*.   See pages 80, 81. — *Note in
Original.*
Mgr Henri-Marie-Dubriel de Ponbirand arrived at Quebec, in August, 1741, and took possession of the office of Bishop on the 30th of

The governor of Canada, is also governor of Louisiana. Although clothed with ample authority for the police of the country, and negotiations with the Indians and foreigners, he is greatly restricted by the intendant, who is absolute master of financial matters, is charged with all the trade and justice, and is at the head of the sovereign council of the country.

The trade of Canada is made on the king's account, and by individuals. The intendant has the general direction of this business. The king has magazines at Quebec, Montreal, St. John, Chambly and Carillon, and for the posts further up at La Presentation, Niagara, Frontenac, the fort at the portage, at Presque Isle, Riviere aux Boeufs, and at Fort Du Quesne.

The magazine at Quebec is a depot to supply that at Montreal, and also issues supplies for trade with our domiciliated Indians, the Abenakis, and others down the river. The magazine at Montreal furnishes merchandises to all the posts above named. Its trade directly with the Indians was but small, until the king appointed a commissary. These magazines furnish all the provisions for the war, as well as for trade and

that month. He died at Montreal June 8, 1760, and to the last was a strong adherent to the French interests. On the day that Quebec capitulated, he addressed a mandate to all the faithful of his diocese, tending to excite a patriotic feeling. He was succeeded by Jean Olivier Briand, who came over as secretary to Ponbirand in 1741, was chosen to be Bishop of Quebec Sept. 11, 1764, went to England, was approved by the king, and after being duly confirmed, returned to Canada in June, 1766. He died June 25, 1794.— *Knox's Journal*, ii, 108; *Liste Chronologique*, p. vi, vii.— ED.

for the king's service   They also in part supply the artillery.

The king has at all these places, store-keepers nominated by the intendant, to whom they report direct. The intendant has under him a commissary of ordnance of the Marine, who remains at Montreal to attend to the details of the upper country.

Munitions, provisions and goods, intended for trade or presents to the Indians, come from France in vessels laden on the king's account. The Bureau of the Marine furnish all these effects, and many therein concerned have doubtless an interest in the purchases.

They send ventures, which amount in every way to the best possible account, and which apparently they pay to the king, over the footing of current merchandizes in Canada. But the greatest evil is, that they send goods which are not proper for the Indian trade, such as large mirrors mounted upon morocco, silk stuffs, and remnants of various other fabrics, handkerchiefs, hose, and in short all the remnants of the shops. The intendant who was attached to the marine, dared not refuse all these articles, and sent them in form to separate stores, where they spoiled, or were stolen, or were turned to other uses. They made reports of consumption at the end of a certain time, and the money paid for them by the king, went into the pockets of those furnishing them, and all the loss was his. We should add to this, the damages unavoidable in a long transportation, and what would be stolen. The furnishers having thus a great profit upon the losses, while the king sustained them, although the profits upon trade in ordinary times was very great, — or otherwise no private persons would have wished to engage in this trade, especially in the most remote and almost inaccessible regions.

The goods for Indian trade, are guns for hunting, lead, balls, powder, steel for striking fire, gun-flints, gun-screws, knives, hatchets, kettles, beads, men's shirts, cloths of blue and red for blankets and petticoats, vermillion and verdigris, red, yellow, green and blue ribbons of English weaving, needles, thread, awls, blue, white and red rateen for making moccasins, woolen blankets, of three points and a half, three, two, and one and a half of Léon cloth, mirrors framed in wood, hats trimmed fine, and in imitation, with variegated plumes in red, yellow, blue and green, hoods for men and children of fringed rateen, galloons, real and imitation, brandy, tobacco, razors for the head, glass in beads made after the fashion of wampum, black wines, paints, &c.

The Indians give in exchange for these goods, the skins of roebucks, stags, bears, beavers, otters, pècans, squirrels, martens, lynxes, foxes, muskrats, woodrats, wolves, caribous and moose. They trade also for bread, pork, salt, prunes, molasses, all kinds of meats, and fish, bear's oil, which they value more than goose oil, and the down of aquatic birds. All these different exchanges, are reduced in value to the beaver skin, which is commonly reckoned as a bottle of brandy of thirty sol. The pound of castor is valued at four livres, ten sol; and skins weigh from two and a half to three pounds. The price of our goods varies with the distance of the locality.

The store keepers at the king's posts, were alone charged with this trade, and accounted the product to the intendant. The commandant had a right to see that the Indians were not cheated, and to take of these goods what he thought necessary for presents. The different interests of these persons often made them disagree. The governor almost always found them wrong and recalled them. To avoid these embarrassments, it was usually enough for them to come to some understanding, when they could conduct their affairs together.

The posts in the interior of the country were assigned to officers in favor. Rank was counted there as nothing. They took with them a store keeper who was to trade on their account. As they had no money, they found merchants at Quebec and Montreal, who supplied upon credit all the goods necessary, which they called equipping them. They agreed upon their prices, and gave peltries to the merchants in return. They had to earn profits for both parties. These officers often had occasion to negotiate for the king with the nations near their posts, and to give them goods as presents. They were paid by the intendant, upon the approval and order of the governor. This occasioned many hypothecated accounts which turned to the most certain profit of these commandants, especially in time of war.

These commandants as well as private traders, were obliged to take out licenses from the governor which cost from four to five hundred livres, in order to be allowed to carry their goods to the posts, and to charge some effects to the king's account. This feature always presented a prominent obstacle to trade and establishments of Canada, as they were obliged to take out these licenses every time they wished to go into the interior of the country. The most distant posts in the north west were the most highly coveted, on account of the abundance and low prices of peltries, and the high price of goods.

A third kind of trade was followed by these traders, or *coureurs de bois*, who, having laden some canoes with merchandize, and halving the licenses, went to the homes of the nations outside of the gates of our posts, where they awaited the Indians in their villages to which they followed them, till their return from the chase, and came back after trading, with their canoes laden, at considerable profit. Those especially who were in condition to purchase goods at first hand, made a fortune very quickly, but to do this, it was necessary to determine to lead a most miserable and painful life. These different traders, upon their return to France, might show an amount of two millions five hundred thousand livres.

To the details here given, M. Pouchot had added some observations upon the value which Canada might have been to France if they had better known its resources, and had improved the great advantages which the soil and situation of the country offered; but as the author had only introduced the subject, and promised at some time to return to it, and to further explain it, and as we have not found these papers with further remarks, we have thought proper to suppress the more early and therefore more superficial and unfinished ones. As for the rest, he advances nothing in these but what the Abbé Raynal has seen and discussed with care in his work, where he has had the courage the first to rise above the unjust prejudices which the public had acquired against the French colonies upon the continent of North America;—prejudices which they were forced to justify in the course of the Memoirs printed in the first volumes of the *Ephémérides du Citoyen*. Because the government had committed faults in the administration of the colony of Canada, ought we to conclude that it was worthless, and that we should congratulate ourselves upon its loss? Such, nevertheless, when reduced, are all the arguments of our economist; a member of the political sect which always takes enthusiasm for reason, and who himself, the slave of his system, makes everything yield to it, and in doing this spares neither paradoxes nor contradiction of words.

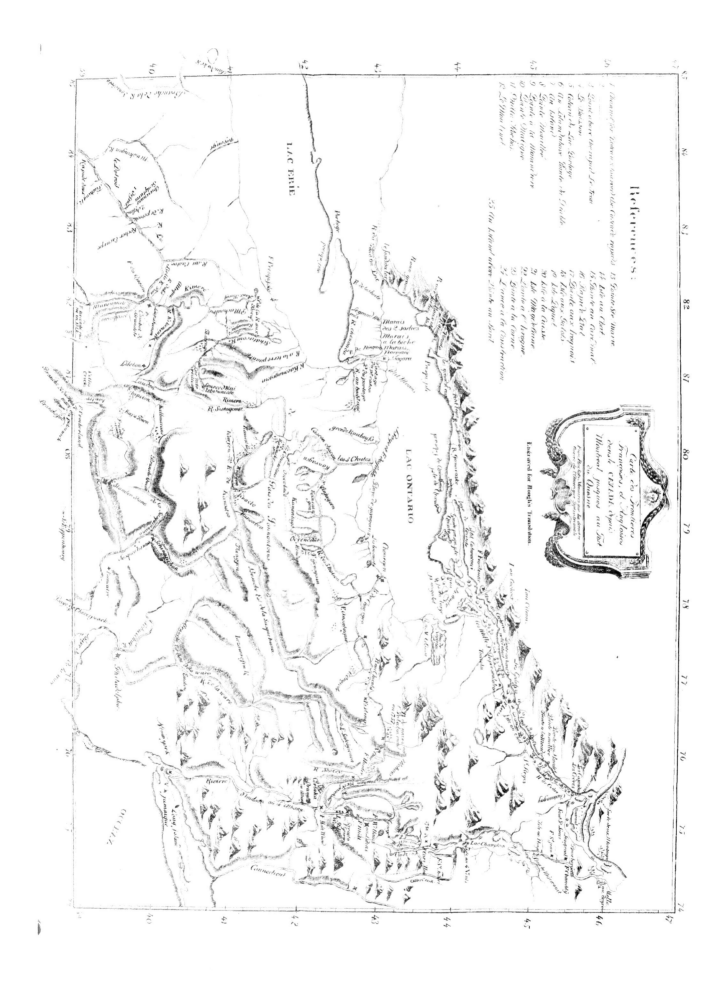

NOTICE.

———

The map which M. Pouchot has drawn, being too large, we have been obliged to reduce it, so that it should have a proportional form to that in which his memoirs are printed. Although that which we give the public, has not preserved the same territory, it comprises, however, the same details, and merits particular attention. As for the rest, the topographical details in some degree supply that which was unavoidable in this reduction.[1] — *Notice in Original.*

———

[1] M. Pouchot's map was engraved for the tenth volume of the *New York Colonial History*, and the engraving was then destroyed. It is reproduced on stone, for the present edition. — ED.

TOPOGRAPHICAL OBSERVATIONS.[1]

M. Pouchot had forgotten nothing in imparting a knowledge of the topography of North America. We have found in his papers, a general description of the continent, imperfect, it is true in some points, but finished, and of unusual accuracy as regards the country which had been the theatre of the late war. He had extracted from that part of his work, the observations we shall present, and which serve to properly explain his map. The great care with which he had prepared it, proves that the description of which we have spoken were quite material, and therefore we have thought it our duty to publish it. We will not, however, deny, that in this description are found details which do not relate to observations chiefly intended to make known the principal communications between Canada and the English colonies, and

---

[1] The third volume of the original work, which begins at this place, is made up of a number of separate subjects which were apparently unfinished essays of the author, collected and published by his editor after his death. We have deemed them all valuable contributions to the history of the period to which they relate, and retain them in their respective order. — Ed.

to serve as a guide to those military men who might some day be employed in that country. The author having written only from the descriptions of others, as to what relates to the parts north and east of Canada, we could less depend upon his accounts, and have therefore suppressed them, without injury to his reputation. As for the rest, he himself confessed that the size and shape of Lakes Huron, Michigan and Superior were not known, and that he had only feeble knowledge of the countries situated to the north and west, north-west of these lakes, and inhabited by the Assiniboins, the Monsonis and the Cristinaux.

MM. de la Verandiere,[1] Canadian officers, penetrated into that country and remained about forty-two years. They went as far as three hundred leagues west of Lake Superior, and discovered many new lakes which led one into another. Perhaps they might have arrived at the South Sea, without meeting those obstacles which oppose all such enterprises, and from which alone we can derive knowledge. The chief difficulties are: First, the want of provisions and resources of every kind. Second, the impossibility of conversing with the natives of the country, whose lan-

---

[1] M. de la Verandiere was sent in 1738, at the desire of the Count de Maurepas to discover the Pacific ocean. His route led through Lake Superior, and thence westward to Lake Winnipeg and up the Assiniboins river, but before he reached the Rocky mountains, his party got entangled in war with Indians of that region, and his convoy was attacked. Towards the end of June the Chevalier de la Verandiere again set out from Montreal upon an expedition to the South seas. — *N. Y. Col. Hist.*, ix, 941, 1060; x, 167. — ED.

guage at a certain distance becomes unintelligible even to the Indians who serve as guides. Third, the disinterestedness rarely found in persons engaged in enterprises of this kind, the most of whom when they have filled their canoes with peltries, so abundant in that country, think only of returning. Fourth, the faithless or enigmatical accounts of the Indians who often seek to deceive and mislead travelers, so that they may perish, and then they can pillage their effects. It may be doubtless hoped, that these obstacles will disappear or diminish in proportion as North America is settled, and the relations between the different parts of the north become then more necessary. This revolution will be the work of the liberty which this vast continent will not be slow to enjoy, if the hopes of all Europe are realized.[1]

———

The various positions in which M. Pouchot, captain in the regiment of Béarn was placed, and the journeys he was obliged to make on the principal lines of communication between the French and English possessions in America, have decided him to give the most exact details upon this subject possible.

We shall see that there are there parts unknown even to the English in the country of the Five Iroquois nations, and shall notice the immense labors they were

---

[1] It will be remembered that these memoirs were printed in 1781, before the American Revolution had been decided. — ED.

obliged to undertake, to come even to the French possessions.

M. Pouchot has not attempted to detail on the map he has prepared, the parts inhabited by the French in Canada, which may be found on other special maps. Neither will he notice particularly the parts inhabited by the English, which are so well given on Mitchel's map[1] and especially on that of Evans which is the best.[2]

He will only attempt to mark the course of the principal rivers which serve as communications to the frontiers, and the principal places which serve them as entrepôts.

---

[1] "A map of the British and French Dominions in North America, with its roads, distances, limits, and extent of the settlements. By Jno Mitchell." Published Feb. 13, 1755, in 8 sheets.— ED.

[2] The map of Canada least defective, that has been published is doubtless that of M. Delisle. After him, Pople, an English geographer, has published one in twenty sheets which includes the whole of North America. M. Bellin has pointed out all their errors: See his remarks — *Hist. de la Nouvelle-France*, tom. v. Although he had at his command the collections of the Marine, he is not himself free of errors. We may blame him for having depended too much upon doubtful observations and old maps, and of not having profited by the discoveries of foreign navigators. The researches of M. Danville have been much more exact. Although his maps of North America are not perfect, they still deserve much praise. He has given an account of his labor in a letter addressed to M. Folkes, and inserted in the *Mercurie*, of March, 1751, p. 150. We cannot deny to Mr. Green the merit of the discussion in his map of America, published in 1753. His fellow countryman, M. Mitchel, has done little besides copying his predecessors, in the eight sheets published in 1755. Mr. Evans had began before him his excellent maps by those of Pennsylvania and New Jersey whose publications dates back to the year 1749.— *Note in Original.*

Canada, although of very great extent, has but few communications with the English colonies as well by the remoteness of the inhabited parts, as on account of countries filled with mountains that are found.

According to the most exact researches, M. Pouchot could learn of only five principal communications, of which he will give a particular account.

1st. From the Canada frontier by way of Lake Champlain.

2d. By the River St. Lawrence, from Montreal to Oswego.

3d. By the Oswego river, to the English possessions.

4th. By Lake Ontario to the English frontiers, by the river Casconchiagon.

5th. From Niagara to the Ohio, and from the Ohio, to Pennsylvania and Virginia.

Before entering upon all of these details, we should speak of the river St. Lawrence from its mouth in the Gulf of that name near to Quebec, but in a few words because this part of the river belongs to naval, rather than to land operations.

At the entrance of the river St. Lawrence, at three leagues south of Cape des Roziers, we find the Bay of Gaspé. It has an opening of about two leagues, and we see it in the distance, on account of the white soil cut into banks which are between its entrance and Cape des Roziers. We may safely approach the bank on the north side of the entrance, where there is a little rock named Fourillon, which at a distance resembles a bateau under sail, tide bearing it away from the shore.

On the south side, where the point still advances into the sea, and where the lands are lower; there are some rocks under water at half a league from the entrance, which are dangerous when their place is not known.

They always anchor on the north side, at three quarters of a league into the bay, in fifty-five fathoms of water, and at gun shot from the shore. The anchorage is not good, because the bottom is sloping.

At four leagues further up, which they call Penouille, the anchorage is very good, and the largest ships can cast anchor there in twelve fathoms and touch the bank. We there find a plateau very proper for building a good fortification.

It is difficult to get out of this bay, because one must wait for a wind quite fresh from the land, without which, the getting out is dangerous, on account of the currents which drive upon the rocks above mentioned.

When we have got out of the bay, and wish to enter the river St. Lawrence, we may safely follow the shore at carbine range in turning Cape des Roziers. Although they say there are some sand banks in this part, we have never found them, although we searched the whole of one day, over every part and very near the land.

Vessels which winter in this bay, can scarcely ascend the St. Lawrence sooner than those which leave Europe at an early period, because the N. E. winds which are quite prevalent in the spring, are against one's getting out of the bay, and throw up the ice there as it comes down the river.

The navigation of the river St. Lawrence, although in itself fine, is yet difficult, unless the winds are in the N. E., the course most favorable for going up the river. Fogs are very prevalent on the river.

There are almost no anchorages on the south side, which is much the finest, and we cannot anchor until we reach St. Barnabé or Bic.

It is very probable that there are on the north side many good anchorages and fine harbors, but that shore is almost unknown to us, and we have but few soundings made by chance, and very imperfectly. We will mention for example, the gulf which we dread like the Charybdis. The English have anchored there, and where we had thought it almost impassible they found a passage nine hundred toises wide.

Vessels of a hundred guns, have gone through the channel north of the Isle of Orleans, where the largest frigates have also passed; and the largest merchant ships have gone up as far as to the rapid below Montreal. This is enough to show how little the shores of this river were known, as these mistakes in our knowledge were in the most frequented places.

M. Pouchot remarked, that the Isle aux Coudres is

well located for defence against vessels going up, by placing batteries upon the crumbling banks opposite the narrowest place.

By also placing batteries of heavy guns upon Cape Tourmene, that point would alone be sufficient to stop vessels, as the current forces them to pass very near. They could not, however, stop there to batter the place on account of this very current, whether the tide be running up or down, and they would run a great risk of injury on the passage. This place, by its position, might be made very respectable, being upon a high rock, scarcely admitting of a landing in its environs.

The position of Quebec is very fine, and like that of Namur. It is even better, but the fortifications are very poorly laid out as regards location, and its range of command is narrow.

The French settlements begin at Cape Mouraska, and extend without interruption to Quebec. The villages are three leagues apart from centre to centre. No villages in Canada are defended, and the houses are all two arpents apart. This is all we can say of the interior of the country, to bring us to countries less known and to the frontiers.

CHAPTER I.

Of the Frontier by Way of Lake Champlain.

There are two routes, from the settlements of Canada to Lake Champlain; one by the River Sorel, which is its outlet into the St. Lawrence, and the other is that by crossing at Montreal to La Prairie, and going by land to Chambly or St. John. The St. Lawrence is three leagues[1] wide between Montreal and La Prairie, a village opposite. From La Prairie to St. John, it is three leagues.[2]

At three quarters of a league from this village, we pass a little river with banks twenty feet apart, and beyond this we come to the drowned prairie, which we name *sarannes*, at this place a league wide. We sink into the mud and water knee deep, but below this the bottom is good. The rest of the way to St. John, is through the woods full of springs, which render the road almost impassable if not kept in repair.

This *saranne* might be drained at a small expense if a slight current was given to the waters of the river of St. Therese, and in the Sorel. The road through the woods would be improved by the same work.

---

[1] The distance in an air line is four miles and a half.— Ed.

[2] Fifteen miles.— Ed.

It is thirty leagues [1] from Montreal to St. John by water. We go down the St. Lawrence fifteen leagues[2] to Sorel at the mouth of the river of this name. It is as large as the Saone near Lyons, and deeper when its waters are high in the spring time. The current is rapid. Barks coming from the St. Lawrence can go up as far as the basin of Chambly.[3] The general direction of its course is N. N. W., and its bends are a quarter or a half of a league apart. It bends considerably four leagues from Chambly,[4] where it runs a little more to the N. E., and in this bend is the greatest current.

Beyond Chambly is a rapid of two leagues, above which to the little village of Sante Therese, the river is quite wide, and full of large stones.[5] It is necessary to be there well guided, so as not to strike the bateaux upon rocks. Above Sainte Therese, they go up by poling to St. John with empty bateaux.[6] The

[1] About one hundred miles.— ED,

[2] Forty-six miles.—ED.

[3] There is now a lock at St. Ours.— ED.

[4] Chambly was a fortified point on the Sorel. The fort, a stone structure, stands at the foot of the rapids, and at the head of navigation from the St. Lawrence. It was built in the Revolutionary war and is still in a state of excellent preservation.

[5] Now surmounted by a canal, from St. John to Chambly.— ED.

[6] St. John is at the foot of steamboat navigation on Lake Champlain, and has always been an important frontier town, ever since the revolution. A little south of the village there is a military establishment where a garrison is kept. The river is bridged at St. John. The mounds of earth that mark the side of the ancient fortifications are in the fields back of the present military works. These

portage is three leagues [1] from St. John to Chambly.
From thence to the lake, the river is much larger and
stiller, and deep enough for large vessels.

The land along this river is very good, and above
St. John it would be excellent if cultivated. It is a
low country full of springs, which loose themselves in
great waters; and a part is covered almost the whole
year. These springs make the river difficult to freeze,
and the ice is always poor.

At five leagues [2] above St. John, we come to the
Isle aux Noix, which the French fortified in 1759.[3]
The river is a gunshot wide all around this island, and
the land and woods in its environs are overflowed at
least two feet when the waters are low. We closed
the river here by a row of piles defended by the
intrenchments on the island. This was the only post
capable of covering the colony, when once the enemy
was master of St. Frederic. They could turn this
place by no other way, nor could they bring their artillery by land. M. Pouchot, in going down to Carillon
in 1758, had pointed out this position to the Chevalier
de Lévis. It could accommodate two or three thousand men in case of need.

localities possess extraordinary historical interest from events that
were of later occurrence than those described by the author.— ED.

[1] Twelve miles.— ED.

[2] Eleven miles.— ED.

[3] The Isle aux Noix, became an important point in the American
Revolution, and has ever since been occupied by the British, as a
military post. The works cover nearly the whole island, and are
quite respectable in point of strength. It contains about 85 acres.—ED.

A league above, we find several islands covered with rushes,[1] but the channel is always good for barques. La Prairie à Boyleau and Pointe au Moulin Foucaut, are the only dry places where camps could be formed conveniently.

When we enter Lake Champlain in a bateau, we take the right to gain Point au Fer,[2] and from thence to Point Skenoncton,[3] from whence we cross to the Valcourt islands. We may follow the west side, but it is very sinuous, and we lose more than two leagues.

A little above the Valcourt Islands on this side is the River Au Sable. We may land everywhere on the first Valcourt island,[4] and in the second there are several fine harbors on the open side well sheltered. In these different creeks more than two hundred bateaux might be placed. The rest of the shores of this island are steep rocks.

Four leagues above, is a kind of rocky cape,[5] with a little bay, where two or three bateaux might find shelter in bad weather.

Opposite, is the Isle au Chapon,[6] a little hook of

---

[1] Ash Island, Hospital Island, &c. — ED.

[2] Point au Fer is in Champlain, Clinton Co., N. Y., on the north side of the mouth of Chazy River. — ED.

[3] Now Cumberland Head. It was sometimes written Squesonton, or Squénonton. It is derived from the Mohawk word *Oughscanoonton*, a deer. — *Tr. Am. Antiq. Soc.*, ii, 340; *N. Y. Col. Hist.*, x, 480. — ED.

[4] Crab Island. — ED.

[5] Near Port Kent. — ED.

[6] Schuyler Island. — ED.

land on the upper side of which we may very conveniently land, and hold bateaux in shelter. All around the rest of this island are only great rocks, which would however afford shelter from the wind. This cape I have mentioned terminates the longest mountains in this quarter.

From the Isle au Chapon, we go to the Point of the Isles des Quatre-vents, and in fine weather we may cross to these islands.[1] In 1759, General Amherst wishing to attack the Isle aux Noix, came with a detachment of five or six thousand men to encamp on this point, but was struck by a N. W. wind which held five or six days, by which he lost a dozen bateaux. The bad season then beginning forced him to return.[2]

We may encamp near a river which is at the head of a bay near Split Rock, to the south. This river takes its rise near Lake St. Sacrament, and some hostile parties have occasionally taken this route to reach Lake Champlain.[3]

Beyond Split Rock, the lake resembles a river, and the surrounding mountains make a very fine basin as

[1] This point is in the town of Willsborough, Essex County, N. Y., and Peru Bay extends up behind it. The islands are now called the Four Brothers. — ED.

[2] The wrecks of these boats may still be seen under water. — ED.

[3] The river answering nearest to this description is the Bonquet River, but the mouth of this stream is some miles north of Split Rock. General Burgoyne's army landed here in the summer of 1777, when on his disastrous campaign that terminated in surrender at Saratoga. From the valley of this river to that of the Schroon a branch of the Hudson, it has been recently proposed to build a railroad. — ED.

far as to St. Frederic. The west side is very mountainous. An inspection of the map will give a better idea of the country than any description. On the east side, there are in this region several fine bays for encamping.

We rarely follow the east side of the lake either in going up or down, and we should remark that in going down, we should keep to the left or west side, or run the risk of getting into Missiskouit Bay. The banks of Lake Champlain are great uninhabited plains. The soil is very good to cultivate, and the timber fine and proper for ship building.

Before the war, the environs of St. Frederic were inhabited. This fort, built as we may see from the map, on a peninsula, was a redoubt of masonry, to which was added a wall of stone without terracing. The surrounding wall was more than two feet thick. M. de Bourlamaque blew up this fort in 1759, when he fell back from Carillon to the Isle aux Noix.

The English have built quite a fort there, upon a spot where a windmill stood. It is a pentagon, about eighty or a hundred toises around, and built entirely of wood. The pieces of the revetment on the outside are three feet square, bound in by heads of timber work, filled with earth, and surrounded by a good fosse.

Upon some small rocks in the vicinity, they have built several redoubts or block houses, after the system of Marshal Saxe. These rocks form a kind of circle around the place. The highest may be thirty feet in elevation, and they fall away with a slope to the country around with very little soil upon them.

The interval from the bay[1] to the river is closed by block houses a hundred toises apart, with a wooden intrenchment between them. This port is much better located for the English than for the French colonies, on account of the difficulty which troops would find in throwing up earth to cover an attack.

Two leagues above St. Frederic, and on the same side is the river á la Barbue.[2] It has a sandy bottom and four feet of water at lowest, or at least seven in the spring. Its bed is all covered with rushes, and very thickly bordered by willows. It has no very plain channel as we can find. The breadth of the stream is a gun shot. The bank from St. Frederic is about forty feet above the water and very uniform, and the woods thin and very open.

In going a league up this river, on the same side, we meet a very high and steep mountain. The course of this river is entirely among these mountains, and quite impassible for an army. Its length is seven or eight leagues.

On the opposite shore is a tongue of land, and the mountains come down to the lake. Quite a large army could encamp there.

The river of Carillon at this place is not more than

---

[1] Bulwagga Bay. — ED.

[2] Putnam's Creek. — ED.

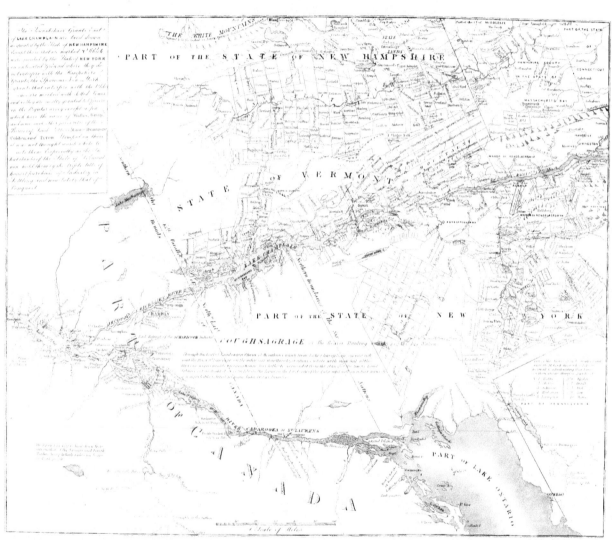

A CHOROGRAPHICAL MAP of the Northern Department of NORTH AMERICA

Drawn from the Latest and most accurate Observations

a gun shot in width, and it is the narrowest place between St. Frederic and Carillon. This post could not be turned to cover St. Frederic. By its rear, it would have communication with that fort. It has a cove or bay which makes up from towards St. Frederic, where bateaux could come without being seen.

Some batteries placed at the angle of the opening I have described, would sweep the river of Carillon as far as to the peninsula. Above, occurs the best position found in the whole course of this river to prevent the passage of Lake Champlain. Large vessels can go up as far as Carillon, and bateaux come up under the Falls.

The English have built a road by land from the Falls to St. Frederic, over which they could take cannon. They have also made a road from Carillon to a fort called Number Four,[1] on the Connecticut. It is thirty-five leagues long, and requires four days to travel it. The militia, returning to New England from their camp near St. Frederic in 1759, took this road, and during the summer they drove by this route the cattle from those provinces, sent for the use of the army.

The fort of Carillon[2] is a square of forty-five toises on a side externally, and is built piece upon piece of timber, fourteen or fifteen inches square. The parapets are twelve feet thick, filled with earth and broken

---

[1] Now Charlestown, Sullivan County, N. H. — ED.

[2] In English *Ticonderoga*, and in Indian *Tcondtaogen.* — *Note in Original.*

stone from the debris of the mountain. Its exterior works are a demi-lune facing the angle of the hill, a fosse of five or six toises wide, with its covered way and a glacis in the rear of the fort, at the end of the bluff. It has also a redoubt, which commands the water.

This fort is built upon a rock very steep almost all around. The side most exposed is commanded by a height where an intrenchment is built, four hundred toises distant. Around this place, upon the front I have described, there is no earth for opening trenches, because it has all been taken off to form the glacis.

By occupying the height of the intrenchment, and opening trenches on the flats by the river, one might attack with success, as there earth could be found to cover; and from Diamond Point,[1] it is very easy to batter the fort with artillery. This post, as well as Carillon, defends the passage of the bay and that of the river of the falls, but it would not hinder from going to St. Frederic by land.

Opposite Carillon is the mountain Serpent-à-Sonnette,[2] from whence also Carillon could be battered by artillery. At the entrance of the bay is a difficult foot path in this mountain which communicates with Lake George or St. Sacrament.

The English have built a fine saw mill at the Falls,

---

[1] Mount Independence on the Vermont side. — ED.

[2] Mount Defiance. — ED.

and a block house with four cannon, and large enough for a hundred men.[1] They have also shortened the portage road at least a quarter of a league.

The road is good, and little liable to dispute, being on the mountain slope which is very gentle, and bounded on one side by the mountain Serpent-à-Sonnette, and on the other by the river of the Falls.

Before reaching the Falls after leaving Carillon, we come to a ravine, which commands almost entirely across the isthmus. It is very deep and steep on the side towards Carillon. On the left there is a hillock,[2] which strikes the passage by the Falls, and on the right the bank commands to a stream, and to the cove of the river of Carillon.

This is the best point to hold with an army, as it covers Carillon and the whole course of the river, and we cannot be seen in reverse, as in the intrenchments that are actually built. The English have cut down nearly all the wood in this part, along the road to the portage, at the foot of Mount Serpent-à-Sonnette and upon Diamond point.

In going to Lake George by the right of the river

---

[1] The outlet of Lake George is three miles long, and the descent is 220 feet. The volume of water passing, is estimated at 4,463 feet per second, and at lowest 400 feet. It is not liable to extremes of high and low water, as the lake is fed by springs. Restrictions upon the title have hitherto prevented the full development of this hydraulic power. — *Cook's Ticonderoga*, 15, 17. — ED.

[2] This is, I believe, Mount Independence. — *Note in Original.*
Mount Independence is on the east side of the lake. — ED.

above the Falls, we find the river Bernes, which is narrow, but deep, and so difficult to pass that it could be defended. In going up, we next meet the current of the Arbres Mataché.

Lake George is scarcely more than a league and a half wide, by sixteen in length. It is surrounded by very steep mountains, especially on the left. In going from Carillon to Fort George, it is almost impassable to persons even on foot. The right side although very bad, is, however, passable. The detachment under the orders of the Chevalier de Lévis passed that way, when they went to invest Fort George in 1757. We had a camp of observation at the entrance upon the lake called the Camp of Coutre-Coeur. It was not well located, because it could be turned by the Arbres Mataché, and by the lake. At this place the English landed in 1758. It was not then occupied.[1]

The position would have been better, had it been a little further advanced, at the foot of Mount Pelée. A post upon this mountain would have been very advantageous, as it could not have been turned by land, but it would have run the risk of being passed by the lake, especially by large vessels.

The north point of the bay of Ganaouski, would be a good place to defend the passage of this lake. A camp there, would be very sure of not being turned.

[1] Since known as How's Landing.— ED.

The lake is very narrow at this point, and by occupying with artillery the two little islands which are near, it would scarcely be possible to cruise upon the lake.

The location of Fort George which we took and destroyed in 1757, was on a kind of neck. The English had fortified its summit to form an intrenched camp, from fear of being turned by the bay, which has a point of defense — the Queen's rock.

The English had begun in 1759, a fort about eighty toises square on the outside. The bottom of the rampart is more than eighteen feet thick and of masonry. The parapet is built piece upon piece, laid very carefully and filled with earth twelve feet thick. In December 1759, it had one bastion finished, all casemated like a redoubt. Probably the rest are planned in the same way. Below, to cover embarkation, there was another much smaller square fort, which the English have built since the demolition of the old one. It is built piece upon piece, and at the top is a fraise sloping a little down with a piece of timber running around to cover the top of the parapet and hold the battlements in their place. The location of the old fort now demolished, is dotted upon the map.

The road of the portage is very good for all kinds of wagons, although the country is quite mountainous, rendering it favorable for ambuscades by the parties which we sent, and which passed by way of the Bay.[1]

[1] South Bay.— ED.

10

Towards the middle of the portage is the hut, which is a little fort of upright timbers to serve as an entrepôt and to favor convoys. It is capable of holding a hundred men. At a league and a half from this fort, the road strikes the Hudson or Orange River and upon its banks at a league and a half beyond, we find the fort called by us *Lydius,* and by the English *Edward.*[1]

This fort is a square of forty or forty-two toises on the outside, with one side upon the river bank. The ditch which surrounds it, is about five toises wide and

FORT EDWARD.

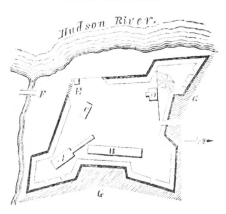

REFERENCES.

A. *Magazine.*
B. *Barracks.*
C. *Storehouse.*
D. *Hospital.*

E. *Flanker at the Watergate.*
F. *Bridge.*
G. *Moat in front of the Parapets.*

---

[1] This fort was sometimes called Fort Lyman, from the officer who constructed it. It was named Fort Edward in honor of Edward, duke of York, grandson of George II, then reigning. The village and town of Fort Edward are named from this fort, the last vestige of which has long since disappeared.— ED.

shallow. The rampart is of earth partly revetted with saucissons, and partly with timbers laid piece upon piece. The parapet is made of coffers of wood filled with earth, with a fraise around the cannon on the flanks, and upon the points of the bastions. The embrasures are closed with Chevaux-de-fraise. A little brook runs along these works at the lower part of the place, which is commanded all around at good range of cannon shot. They have there built several blockhouses to cover, and thus form an intrenched camp. On the island before the place [1] is a poor intrenchment, quite commanded on every side, and several groups of barracks.

The blockhouses of which we have spoken, are redoubts of wood, consisting of two squares. The best are those of St. Frederic. They have a ditch fifteen feet wide, and the earth thrown out is made into a glacis. A stockade is built obliquely along the ridge. The first story is loop-holed, and serves for the guard. In the upper part, the angles of the square correspond with the middle of the square faces below, which gives the structure an octagonal form. There are usually some embrasures for cannon in the upper part, besides loop-holes.

The country around Fort Edward, although hilly, appears proper for cultivation. The landscape is very pleasant, being upon high ground.

---

[1] Monroe's Island.— ED.

The river is not navigable a league above this fort
on account of its swiftness, and it there comes out of
the great mountains.[1] It is there only a gunshot
across and quite deep. At a quarter of a league below Fort Edward, we cross the river upon a wooden
bridge, and the road continues through a low and
marshy country for a league. Two leagues still beyond to Fort Miller, they turn down to one side
where they have cut down trees to build the road.
The earth being washed away by the river, had to be
covered at considerable cost with round pieces of
wood, to make it firm.

Fort Miller is a little square for holding two hundred men, and is built partly of earth and partly of
timber, placed piece upon piece. It appeared to be
newly built, and was not finished when M. Pouchot
passed there. It is in low ground, marshy and
muddy. They join the river at a gun shot distance
from this fort, which is the beginning of the road
above described.

It is called twelve miles from Fort Miller to Saratoga or Saracto. At a league and a half before reaching this fort, the river passes between two high hills,[2]
which form a good post. The mountains to the right

---

[1] Glen's Falls.— ED.

[2] By this defile the unlucky Burgoyne counted upon making his
retreat, but the Americans having got before him, he was forced to
sign on the 17th of October, 1777, the capitulation of which the public
is informed.—*Note in Original.*

and left of this valley are quite elevated, and the waters of the river are fine.

Saratoga[1] is at the end of a flat in a bend of the river. It is built of earth revetted with saucissons, and will hold a garrison of three hundred men. There is a bank at cannon shot from the fort which commands it. It is a bushy ridge of gravel and stones.

From Saratoga, we continue to follow the river through a kind of meadow or pasture ground. We meet two falls of water upon this route to Stillwater. At the first are some saw mills, and they were building some bateaux. We can come very near to the Falls by water, and embark immediately below. It is the same at the second fall.

Stillwater[2] is a little smaller than Saratoga, and built in the same manner, being only a large star redoubt of earth revetted with saucissons, with a ditch eighteen feet wide, fraised. This fort is in a meadow, and commanded at gun shot distance by a terrace which surrounds it, and behind which could be placed three or four thousand men, which renders the place very bad. It is an entrepôt of provisions and other

[1] On the East bank of the Hudson in the present town of Easton, Washington County.— ED.

[2] At Stillwater a stockaded fort was erected on the elevated ground at the north end of the village, about where the Presbyterian church now stands. And on the flat below this, a few rods from the river, were the store houses,— two long buildings which were kept in good repair, and continued to be used in the public service through the revolutionary war.— Tr. N. Y. Ag. Soc., 1848, p. 912.— ED.

goods going up from Albany, to be carried to Fort
George. They come up from that city by water in
flat bottomed bateaux resembling ferry scows, but
which have sails.

The tide comes up to this place. The carriages from
this place are by land, on account of the two falls,
and some sand bars which are found along the river.
It is otherwise large enough, with a good and deep
current.

The entrepôt for wagons carrying stores from Stillwater to Fort George, is at a place called Half-Moon,
where in 1759 four hundred wagons were collected
for the service of the army, being paid twelve livres a
day, and the men and teams fed, whether employed
or not.

From Fort Edward to Stillwater, the valley is shut
in with mountains towards the Connecticut. The
slopes although steep, are however susceptible of
tillage. There is a road from Fort Edward leading
to the Connecticut and to Boston.

The mountains begin to fall off at Stillwater, and
the country is there cultivated. Half-moon is a poor
redoubt, at the end of a flat at the confluence of the
Mohawk River which here forms a semi-circle, which
has given name to the place.

At the end of the flat, which may be a quarter of a
league, we go up quite a steep hill, and two miles
beyond cross the Angiers or Mohawk River in a scow,
half a league above the falls in that river. Upon the

side opposite the ferry a redoubt was begun for four pieces to cover this passage against our parties. The fall of this river is fine seventy-five feet high,[1] and almost perpendicular.

The road for the next two leagues winds among the hills to reach the bottom of the Hudson valley, and this part is very favorable for ambuscades.

When we reach the foot of the hills, we then follow the bank of the Hudson, along the foot of little hills which are quite steep. They are higher on the other side of the river.

Just beyond the suburb of Orange, we pass upon a bridge, over a stream[2] upon which are several mills. Albany, or Orange, is built upon the slope of a hill which borders the River Hudson, otherwise called Albany or Orange. It is the form of a triangle, the base of which is a fine quay along the river, with jettees, forming a very fine port. Barques, snows and schooners, come up from the sea as far as Albany, at which place they do a good trade.

At the apex of the triangle, is a citadel revetted

---

[1] And not fifty, as M. Buffon wrote.— *Hist. Nat.* I, i, p. 89..— *Note in Original*.

This cascade at the present village of Cohoes, Albany Co., has been since greatly reduced in volume by the withdrawal of its waters for the enlarged Erie Canal, and for hydraulic power, in the extensive manufactories that have been erected there. In time of high water, they, however, present a spectacle of much grandeur. The Albany Northern Rail Road crosses the river a short distance below.— ED.

[2] Patroon's creek, now chiefly used to supply the Albany city water works.— ED.

with stone.[1]   It is square, forty toises on a side externally, with a single ditch twenty feet wide, and without
a glacis.   It is commanded and may be approached
from the south by some hollows to within pistol shot.

There is by the side of the city a very fine hospital,[2]
built of wood by General London, and sufficient to
accommodate fifteen hundred sick.   The streets of
Albany are fine, wide, well arranged and well alligned,
but without pavements, which renders them very
muddy.   The houses are regularly built in the Flemish
style.   The city may contain five or six thousand souls,
mostly of Dutch or Flemish origin.

On the north side of the city we find a deep ravine,
which takes its origin near the citadel.   It is fortified
along its border by a good fosse and a palisade.   The
rest of the place is surrounded by large upright timbers, about a foot in diameter, and fifteen or sixteen
feet high.   Notwithstanding all this, the place is not
sheltered against a surprise.   From the other side of
the river a very good road leads from Orange to the
Connecticut and to Boston.

The Hudson River is a good quarter of a league
wide, and retains this breadth as far down as to the
Isinglas Mountains.[3]   Its current is gentle, and its

---

[1] Fort Frederic, built in what is now State Street, opposite St.
Peter's church.— ED.

[2] This hospital stood a little north of the fort near the present site
of the Lutheran church. — ED.

[3] The Highlands. — ED.

depth good, with but few shallows. Perhaps no navigation is more sure, as the vessels that go up from New York to Albany, have usually but three men for a crew. There is almost anywhere good bottom for anchorage either on the east or west side, and they can go where they please according to the wind.

The banks on each side are high, and form a chain of hills covered with poor soil. The dwellings are separated by intervals of about three quarters of a league. Except some houses in particular places, the country has a poor and desert-like aspect, like the poor countries in our mountains in Europe.

We find some mouths of streams along the course of this river, which appear to be not navigable, and some mean villages. They say that the interior of the country along these streams is better settled, especially along the Sopus river.[1] The country however, promises nothing fine, being very mountainous and filled with great boulders or detached rocks.

At six leagues below Albany, we find two islands which form bars across the river, so that loaded vessels can only pass at full tide. There are two channels; the one goes to the right of the left hand island, and then turns very short, being the worst of the two channels. The other is between the right hand island and the west shore, where there is a village.[2] They then

[1] Rondout River. — ED.

[2] Coxsackie. The navigation near this place and above still continues bad on account of the bars that form in the river. Large sums

11

go right towards this village, turn towards the island, and then coast along it.

Although this navigation is much used, vessels often ground here, but without injury to the boat. They call it the Devil's bar. This is the only difficulty worth noticing that is met with in this navigation. It is curious to see the prodigious quantity of sturgeon who are constantly springing from the water in the summer season.

At twelve leagues below this passage, we see on the right a group of large mountains called Kaatskills, which extend far away into the upper parts of Pennsylvania. They are higher than in those regions, and are scarcely second to our Alps except that they do not retain their snows in summer.[1] They are very steep, and nothing but simple rocks covered with woods.

At fifteen leagues beyond, we enter the mountains called Isinglas,[2] which although not so high are almost vertical on the river. They usually form chains of rock, covered with poor wood, of which considerable quantities are sold in New York.

_____

of money have been spent in removing them and in building dykes to deepen and straighten the channel, the effect of which has generally been to only shift the bar to another place. In a river where the tide and current meet, these troubles must always necessarily occur. — ED.

[1] The elevation of the Catskill Mountains is far less than that stated by the author. High Peak is 3,718, and Round Top 3,804 feet above the Hudson. — ED.

[2] As we enter the Highlands from above, Butter Hill on the right is 1,520, and New Bacon on the left is 1,685 feet high. — ED.

We wind among the curves in these mountains about four leagues. We find some anchorages in lucky places for shelter, but if these are lost, one would be in danger in bad weather. The river still preserves about its same breadth, and the current is so strong that they only go with the tides, which are very strong, both up and down. They lay at anchor when the tide is against them, through the whole course of this navigation, unless they have a good wind which can enable them to overcome its current.

This forms a division of the country, which may be called the upper and the lower regions. There are here some very good points for cutting off communication from the lower country and the sea. At the entrance of this gorge is a little island which would very well bar the river, and is not itself commanded from the land.[1]

In coming out of the mountains, the river forms on the left a little bay, which in coming up might be readily mistaken for the river channel on account of its opening between the rocks.[2] After coming out, the country to the right for two or three leagues presents very high banks.

The country, after leaving the mountains, is very

---

[1] Pollopel Island opposite New Windsor. — ED.

[2] Peekskill Creek. The illusion described in the text is very striking, and one could scarcely doubt at a mile distance, in coming up, but that the channel was about to turn to the right, instead of the left. — ED.

agreeable, and appears like a fine plain with pleasant landscapes, well cultivated and occupied with well built houses. The river is usually a league wide from this outlet to New York.

This chain of mountains which we have described, extends east and west along the whole of the English provinces, at about the same distance from the sea, preventing the other rivers of these countries from communicating between the coast and the interior of the continent, as we shall see hereafter.

The Hudson River is the only one that furnishes a profitable navigation with the interior of the country, and where the tides stop, we find ourselves above the sources of the Delaware and the Susquehanna.[1]

The route of this river, forms without doubt, the finest entrance to that part of the continent of America called *Canada*, as it can be used the year through, to communicate with Europe, which is not the case with the St. Lawrence. By way of the Mohawk River, we find ourselves without much difficulty in the midst of the lands and the lakes.

The province of New York embraces the whole course of the Hudson River and twenty miles on each side, the whole length of the Mohawk, and also Long Island. New York or Menede, is a very fine city, on a kind of island formed by a little branch from the Hudson which falls into an arm of the sea which sepa-

---

[1] An important observation in judging of the elevation and the land-slopes of the continent of North America. — *Note in Original.*

SOUTH-WEST VIEW OF THE CITY OF NEW YORK.

rates it from Long Island and the main land. The streets of this city are very wide, all paved, and some of them ornamented with rows of trees. The houses are in the Dutch style, many of them of wood and of fine construction. The city is thrifty and quite commercial, and every one has an easy air. There are about fifteen or eighteen thousand souls.[1]

The principal harbor which is on the side towards Long Island, is always full of merchant ships which come and go continually, and there are usually two hundred and fifty or three hundred in port. Vessels of more than thirty guns cannot anchor there. It is a little deeper on the Hudson River side, yet it is much less frequented, because it is not there sheltered from the south winds. The bars that we meet near Sandy Hook, doubtless would prevent vessels of the greatest force from coming up the river.

At New York they have coast pilots, for conducting vessels from Sandy Hook to the city, for which the charges are very high. Along the quays of this city, they have constructed piers to receive the vessels which come up directly to the shore, and unload by planks or flying bridges.

This city is not fortified,[2] and has only a citadel at

---

[1] This estimate is very nearly correct as referring to 1768. In 1756, the population of the island was 13,046, and in 1771, 21,862. The two steel plate views of the city, which we here give, were made from sketches dated the same year that these memoirs were written. — ED.

[2] We should remember that the author is speaking of the state of the country as it was in the late war. — *Note in Original.*

the point of the two passages. This is square, and
about sixty toises on the outside, revetted in good
masonry, without ditch or covered way. It is well
fortified with cannon. At the front, which is on the
point of land, they have built upon some notches in
the rocks, a wall twelve feet thick, which forms an
intrenchment and a kind of false-braye to the citadel,
where they have ninety pieces of cannon in battery, of
from twelve to twenty-four pound balls. The platforms are all of large flat stones. These pieces are
mounted on marine carriages, and sweep not only the
bay, but a small island used as a hospital for the Quar-
antine.[1]

Vessels can go up the river by bearing a little to the
west side, and they can land above the city, which is
only defended against the country by some upright
timbers like those of Orange. The place is capable of
being well fortified, having only one front on the land
side, which is very favorable for defense. This place
gives naturally cross fires on the low grounds in its
front, and its sides being elevated commands the river
at an elevation of thirty or forty feet.

Ships of war can only come up to Sandy Hook,[2] ten

A fort had existed at the lower point of the island for more than
a century before this period. Its name was usually changed to that
of the reigning sovereign, and it was then called Fort George. — ED.

[1] Governor's Island. — ED.

[2] Admiral Howe in 1778 found that he could come and anchor much
further up. — *Note in Original.*

or twelve leagues below New York. The anchorage there is very good, and sheltered from the south winds by the hills which form the cape. There occurs at that place a great reef, which runs out into the open sea from Long Island, and obliges vessels in coming up to gain this anchorage, and the same precautions are necessary in going out.

In coming from the sea, they bring the Cape in line with these hills, when they come towards the Sandy point which they approach to within gun shot, always with sounding-lead in hand. As soon as they have passed this point, they find good bottom.

When they wish to go up the river to reach Staten Island, they have also several turns to make. They must pass near the Jersey shore a little way, then follow N. E. of the Island, and then keep in the middle of the river to the upper part of the arm of the sea where the citadel stands, where they enter this arm, which is the port. In coming from Rhode Island to New York by this arm, we find a narrow strait called Heltgat, which must be passed at full tide, on account of the currents and whirlpools which form there, and cast the vessels upon the rocks. It is three leagues above New York.

Above Staten Island, we come to a small island with a country seat upon it. This would be a very proper place for a depôt.[1]

---

[1] Bedlow's Island, now covered by Fort Wood.— Ed.

The country to the east of New York, in going to Connecticut, is full of little hills, and is well cultivated. I will not go into details concerning those parts, and will only say, that they are all usually divided into counties or shires, that the houses are very scattered, and that there is to each three hundred arpents of land. They limit the one to the other in every sense. The cities, or chief places of each county, are groups of houses with nothing of particular note.

When the government of each province raises its militia, they are not held more than six months at a time. They only issue papers to the officers for this time, which does not give them much importance among them, and after a man who has been an officer in one campaign, he will return as a soldier in the next, and then again an officer, &c.

All the inhabitants are classed into companies of a hundred men. When they form battalions, they are made up of a certain number of men from each of these companies. Each inhabitant may put a substitute in his place, whom he pays for the six months campaign, from May to the 1st of November. Some have given as high as eighty piastres to their substitutes, and several assured M. Pouchot, that they had received as much as twelve or fifteen hundred livres. The militia are mostly composed of people hired in this way.

One may judge of the population of these countries from the following details. During the war against

SOUTH EAST VIEW OF THE CITY OF NEW YORK

Canada, they raised twelve men from each company,
New England and Connecticut furnished 7,000, New
York 2,300, New Jersey 3,000 and the other colonies
in proportion.

Long Island is two, three, and four and five leagues
wide, and thirty long. Half of the island, especially
that towards New York, is level, very thrifty and well
settled; and although the soil is a gravelly sand, it is
fertile. The remainder is more hilly and not as fertile. They sow some wheat, but much more Indian
corn. They raise many fine cattle and furnish large
quantities of salted meats for the American Islands.
There are as many inhabitants in this island alone, as
in all Canada.[1]

They do not sow much wheat in the provinces of
New England and Connecticut, but they raise a prodigious quantity of cattle, with which they trade ex-
tensively with the islands.

New Jersey is a magazine of grains. This province is almost entirely level, filled with little tidal
streams, which greatly facilitate the importation and

---

[1] This is a mistake. M. Pouchot states in a MS. note that there are
about 30,000 souls on Long Island, while in Canada we reckoned in
the last war more than 90,000. — *Note in Original.*

From Bouchette and other authorities, we prepare the following
summary of the population of Canada at different periods :

In 1660, 3,418 ;— in 1676, 8,415 ;— in 1688, 11,246 ;— in 1700, 20,000 ;
— in 1706, 20,000 ;— in 1714, 26,904 ;— in 1759, 65,000 ;— in 1784,
113,000. A capitation list of Canada in 1754, gave Quebec 8,000,
Montreal 4,000, Three Rivers and the Forges 800, the rural districts
42,200, and all Canada 55,000.— *N. Y. Col. Hist.*, x, 271. Long Island
had a population of 23,783 in 1756 and 27,731 in 1771.— ED.

exportation of commodities. They also raise many cattle. There are mines of iron and copper, and foundries of artillery for the use of their merchant vessels. There are no large rivers in this province, but many fine harbors, surrounded by woods, where they say the largest vessels can anchor.

As regards the Connecticut river, although deep enough and with a gentle current, it is still of but little use. The tides do not extend far up into the land.[1] Besides this there are four or five falls or rapids, where it is necessary to make portages.

The Delaware serves for navigation to the interior of Pennsylvania, yet is scarcely less difficult than the Connecticut, and it has no communication with any frontier of Canada. The same is true of the Schuylkill river, which is shallow and has many rapids.

In the province of Pennsylvania, large vessels go up the Delaware bay to within five leagues of Philadelphia.

The Loup nation came down from near the sources of these two rivers to attack the English settlements of this province, and they did much mischief, being very scattered along the whole frontiers of the inhabited parts.

---

[1] The tides ascend the river to Hartford, about fifty miles.— ED.

CHAPTER II.

OF THE RIVER ST. LAWRENCE, FROM MONTREAL TO OSWEGO.

Although the River St. Lawrence is very well known, its navigation from Montreal where the rapids begin, to Lake Ontario has heretofore been but superficially described. We will now give a minute detail of this passage, and of some of the difficulties that are encountered.

We will observe in the beginning, that the river is only navigable from about the 15th of April, when the ice breaks up. It is usually the full moon of March that decides the season, according as it is earlier or later.

The rivers begin to freeze in Canada about the 1st of December, sometimes sooner when the winds are N. W., but the ice is usually not good before Epiphany.

During the general freezing, we may go from Quebec to Montreal and the Cedars with all kinds of freight even artillery, upon the ice of the river, excepting in the rapids where it never freezes. But in these parts they have built excellent roads upon the land.

This freighting done in winter, would gain fifteen days of time for the navigation of the upper country, because Lake St. Francis[1] breaks up before the river, and as soon as this lake is free, we may sometimes in forty-eight hours make the voyage to Frontenac. This is on account of the difference of climate.

From Quebec to Montreal we do not find much difficulty in the navigation, except at the Rapids of Richelieu, where the tides cease to be felt. They may be ascended with a good wind.[2]

The winds are more frequently from the S. W. than the N. E. in Canada, which renders the navigation longer in going up in some places than in returning. We may anchor anywhere in the river, for we often meet islands where we can find shelter from the winds.

Frigates can go up as far as Sorel, and large merchant ships as far as the rapids of St. Marie, a quarter of a league below Montreal. They can anchor between Ste Héleine Island and the north shore.

Vessels are sometimes fifteen days and even a month waiting for a N. E. wind strong enough to help them up the rapid. The common navigation between Quebec and Montreal is by schooners.

Montreal, from its position, would be susceptible of a good fortification, on account of a stream and low grounds between the city and the mountain. It is, however, commanded at good cannon shot by a hill,

---

[1] This lake is properly only an enlargement of the river. — *Note in Original.*

[2] By the aid of steam tugs, ships can now readily ascend with a head wind. — ED.

which is at the foot of the mountain. But this place, being the centre of the colony has no need of any defense than the island itself.

This place is surrounded by a wall without terraces, three or four feet thick at the bottom, and reduced to eighteen inches at the top. The plan signifies nothing, and its only benefit is to shelter against a surprise.

The island of Montreal is susceptible of defence, because we cannot land everywhere on account of the rapids and currents which occur around it. Its position is admirable on account of the beauty of its scenery in the environs, which are very wide plains. It is of the highest importance, because it is a necessary entrepôt, where the navigation changes from the St. Lawrence to the Outaouais, or the great river.

The second rapid which we find, is that of the Sault St. Louis, two leagues above Montreal. It continues a league, and the voyageurs regard it as the worst in the whole river up to La Presentation.[1] They go up with empty bateaux on the north side, and pass with difficulty through a channel made near a mill, which they call La Chine, belonging to the Sulpicians. This leads to a place higher up, where they have made a general entrepôt with magazines, and where they leave the goods that have to be sent by land from Montreal to the village of La Chine.

---

[1] The lockage up to Lake St. Louis, by the enlarged Lachine canal is 44 feet 9 inches by five locks, and the distance is a little over seven miles across a bend of the river. — ED.

The road of this portage is very poor on account of the mud, especially in the spring, when the wagons are more numerous. This road would be very good if they should make ditches to drain off the water. This neglect has occasioned a large expense in wagoning, and leads to much delay and embarrassment.

If the country were better settled, we could make a canal from La Chine to Montreal, along the little stream which enters between the hill and the city, and which would lead to below the rapid of St. Marie, and avoid the portage of three leagues.

The bateaux used for the navigation of the upper part of this river, carry six thousand pounds, and are of a peculiar form to enable them to resist the efforts made to take them up the rapids. Those that the English built at the latter place, were larger and lighter, but could not endure this navigation after the first voyages. They were always filled with water by the efforts made to keep them up, and those of the French did much better service. The English did not furnish their bateaux with sails, which are very essential on good occasions, but they provided good ash oars while the French used those of pine, which were poor, badly made, and used up in great numbers.

Bateaux leaving La Chine, follow the north side to within a league of the church at Point Claire. They always go up by poling on account of the currents, which are strong, especially around the points of land.

If they wish to pass by Chateaugay, they cross over

at the point. If they wish to pass to the point of the Isle Perraut, they gain the church of Point Claire. From the Isle Perraut they cross to the Cascades. The first that they meet, is where the river makes a little fall across its whole breadth.

Near the land on the west side marked 1 on the map, there is a gutter in the rocks which forms this fall through which the bateaux pass in ascending. Some men on the rocks hold the bateaux by hand, being waist deep in the water. From thence they are taken by towing and poling, a gun shot further up, where there is another rapid, but not so bad as the former.

In going down, we may leap the falls, when we know the two passages on the east, opposite the island. Commonly, however, they go down through the gutter where the bateaux go up.

The third rapid is the Trou, where they half un-load the bateaux, and carry the goods a hundred and fifty paces above this point of rocks. In going up, they pass the bateaux quite against the point of land marked 3. It is necessary to hold the bateau by a rope drawn by several men, while others jump shoulder deep into the water to make it advance in turning this point.

The river is encumbered at this place by large rocks under the water, which falls against them boil-ing like an abyss.

One of these especially, forms a great cavity by the

side of which a thread of water is thrown up by com-
pression into a ridge, down which they pass in descending.   If they miss this passage, they fall into
these gulfs, and can scarcely escape ;—which has given
it the name of the *Trou*.[1]   These different rapids are
called the Cascades.

At a league below the village of Cedars, is a point
of land where the river boils extremely.   It is necessary to make the bateaux in going up, pass very near
the land.   They have there made a channel, to escape
these great currents, but it is not finished, and is
often without sufficient water, and hinders more than
it does good.   The passage marked 4, is named the
Buisson,[2] and is more tedious to the canoe men on
account of the shallow water.   From this they pole
up the bateaux to below the Cedars where they land
the goods to carry them half a league by land above
this village, while they draw up the bateaux by towing.   Some men go into the water to hold them,
especially around a mill belonging to M. de Longueil.
There are some very bad shallows here, because the
river is not deep, and runs upon great boulders or
rocks, which render the passage dangerous and difficult in descending.

Above the mill is another shallow, but not so bad
as the former.   If, at the place where the mill stands,
they had made a little canal inside of the islet upon

[1] A trough or hole.— ED.

[2] The Thicket.— ED.

which it is placed, it would have saved the voyageurs much trouble.

The spot where the church of the Cedars stands, would be very favorable for a fortified post at the head of the rapids. The land there forms a natural fortification, and we find plenty of land easy to dig.[1]

A camp placed at this point, would well cover this approach of the colony. The enemy absolutely could not descend the river under this post, and they would be obliged to make a passage by land through the woods at least four leagues on the side of Vaudreuil. It is not to be supposed they would venture to do this and leave this post in their rear.

From the point of reëmbarkation, they go up by poling to the portage of Coteau du Lac, marked 5. This is a point of land where the water is so broken and boils so strongly, that we are there obliged to unload the bateaux. The portage is sixty paces. It is necessary to get into the water to make the bateaux ascend, and to turn this point.

Above this they cross with oars to gain another point called Point du Diable, which they pass by towing. If, unfortunately, the bateau lurches[2] at this point, the current carries it into the great cauldrons,

---

[1] The English have since built a fort at the Cedars, where Major Sherburne could not long resist an attack in 1776, after the raising of the siege of Quebec by the Americans, who were afterwards masters of this fort.— *Note in Original.*

[2] They call it lurching [embarder] when the currents strike the boat obliquely, when it is impossible to retain it, and it must be left to run the rapids.— *Note in Original.*

and it is inevitably lost. This has happened to voyageurs who have attempted to pass this place by poling.

The island marked 6, above this dangerous place, is extremely advantageous for defending the rapids, either right or left, and in going up or down. It can be landed upon either from above or below, and is altogether one of the best places to defend in the colony. The enemy could not use the river, nor could they carry their bateaux from thence through the woods to the foot of the Cedars. This island is well wooded, and sufficiently large.

The bateaux go by poling along Coteau du Lac, using oars in some places. The current is very strong, and the banks encumbered with trees that have fallen into the water. The island marked 7, is remarkable, because in going down the Coteau du Lac it is necessary to find a current which is directly opposite this island, where the passage occurs for going down to the Cedars ; otherwise they would fall into the great cauldrons, where they must perish without remedy.

The army of General Amherst, in going down to Montreal, from the want of proper guides, lost in this passage eighty common bateaux and four bateaux called carcassieres, carrying each one twelve pound cannon. If he had but four men in each bateau in going down, at least three hundred and thirty-six men must have perished.[1]

---

[1] The Beauharnois Canal, on the south side, in a distance of twelve miles, surmounts an elevation of eighty-four feet, between Lake St.

Lake St. Francis is seven leagues long, and three or four wide.[1] At the entrance of the lake we find Bateau bay, on the north side, which is the side they always follow. From thence they go with oars or sails. Two leagues further up we find Point au Banc, which is a usual camping place. The land there is very good, and there are there some good houses.

If we do not stop at this place, we must cross the lake to find a camping ground, because the bays are deep, and the country all covered with water. Point Mouillée, marked 8, is the end of a meadow which extends into the lake. The country is covered with water, and they sometimes halt there.

Further on we find Pointe a la Morandiere, marked 9. It is a tongue of land where we may encamp, but only with a few people, the spot being small. The woods on this north side are cedars and pines, of which the roots are nearly all the time under water. The whole interior of the land here is greatly encumbered by dead and fallen trees.

From Pointe a la Morandiere, they always navigate through rushes. We must always follow the north shore without getting too near the land, in order to find the best channel of the river. We pass through the rushes between some fine islands called the *Cheneaux*, and at the beginning of these islands cross to the south

Louis and Lake St. Francis by nine locks. It comes out into Lake St. Francis above the bateau rapids. — ED.

[1] About twenty-seven miles long, and from one to five wide. — ED.

if we wish to visit the mission of St. Regis lately founded by the Jesuits[1] and very small in numbers. The lands in the vicinity are fine for cultivation, and it is a very good country for hunting.

Opposite St. Regis, on the side usually followed, the land is quite high, and in going up we find a very abrupt and double point, called *Pointe Maligne*,[2] marked 10, where it is necessary to put on a towing line. Beyond this we reach the *Mille Roches*, marked 11. This is a fall of the waters of the Long Saut by a narrow channel, and from thence passes to the north. The river, which makes a great bend at this place, is much encumbered by great rocks. They have made a channel so as not to be obliged to go around them.[3]

At the entrance of *Mille Roches*,[4] we find the lower point of an island,[5] which we pass on the north side in going up, but on the south in descending the Long Saut. We may land on this island by the lower side, and if supplied with marksmen might easily prevent bateaux from descending.

[1] Founded by Antoine Gordon, a Jesuit, with a party from Caughnawaga. The details are given in the *Hist. of St. Lawrence and Franklin Counties*. — ED.

[2] Just above the present village of Cornwall. — ED.

[3] The Cornwall Canal, beginning just below that town, and following up the north bank to Dickinson's landing, opposite the Long Saut Island, now enables vessels to surmount the Long Saut rapid. This canal is about eleven miles long, and rises forty-eight feet, by the help of six locks. — ED.

[4] The north channel opposite Sheik's Island, close under the north shore, a canal for steamers and small vessels is now built there. — ED.

[5] Sheik's Island on modern maps. — ED.

From Mille Roches we go to *Moulinet*[1] marked 12. We there turn two small islands (where the water is very still), and enter an arm of the river which is very rough. Besides using poles, they are obliged to get into the water shoulder deep to make the bateaux advance. They have there made a channel for passing. We then gain a little island on the right, and come to the foot of the Long Saut.

The Long Saut is a full quarter of a league in length on the north, and three leagues in length descending on the south. The waters boil like the sea in a tempest. Although the current is very rapid in the north passage, they nevertheless bring up the bateaux by towing with four or six men to a line, and two in the bateau to guide it. Fortunately the currents always bear towards the shore. There are some rocks in the channel which renders this passage difficult. They might be taken out, and a road made along the side to greatly lessen the labor of towing. They usually encamp at the head of the Long Saut. This country is full of very fine wood, and would be very proper to cultivate.

The river above the Long Saut has a very strong current, especially around the points of land which we often meet, and where we must always use the poles vigorously. No. 13 is Pointe Ste Marie, one of the most remarkable of these. No. 14, is the *Isle au Chat*,[2]

---

[1] Now Dixon's Mills. — ED.

[2] Still called by this name. It is the town of Louisville. — ED.

noted for being the place where we cross under this island to the south, in going down the Long Saut.[1]

On the island below,[2] there is a point from whence both the north and south channels might be raked by artillery, and a camp might be formed.

No. 15, is *Pointe au Cardinal*, equally noted for its strong current, besides which trees have fallen from the bank, very much hindering the navigation.

No. 16, is the *Rapide Plat*, the currents being of great strength, but not dangerous either in going up or down.[3] We find there a great eddy, which we take to the foot, and then go up by poling, so as not to lurch.[4]

No. 17, is *Pointe aux Iroquoise.*[5] It is not very rough, and is chiefly noted for being a place where they almost always stop, either in going up or down.

[1] Just below Isle au Chat, there is now a short piece of canal with a lock of three feet six inches, to surmount a rapid around Ferren's Point. — ED.

[2] Chrysler's Island. Just below this, on the north side a small fort was erected in the war of 1812-15, to command the channel. It was called Fort Ingles.— ED.

[3] The Rapide Plat canal is four miles long, with a lock of eleven feet six inches.— ED.

[4] The Junction canal along the north shore begins below Point Iroquois, is about seven miles long, and has two locks, together amounting to fourteen feet nine inches. The river is navigable from the head of this canal to Lake Ontario. The total rise from tide water to Kingston at the outlet of the lake is 234 feet.— ED.

[5] Still known by this name on the maps, but locally pronounced "Point Rockaway." It is in the town of Waddington, St. Lawrence Co., just above Ogden's Island.— ED.

The Galots are two very strong checks, and the river across its whole breadth descends in boiling waves.

They follow the shore of the first rapid, and when they come near a kind of jette of rock they put out the towing lines. Great care must be taken to hold the forward end of the bateau towards the shore if you do not wish it taken by the current. The second, above, is not so long. At a gun shot above is a bay called *Aux Perches*, because here the poles are left.

There are no more rapids, and henceforth they need only oars and sails. In going down the Galots, they follow the middle of the current.

No. 18, opposite this bay is the *Isle aux Galots* which may be seven hundred toises around. It can scarcely be landed upon, except above, along a distance of 150 toises on account of the currents meeting below. This island having a good range on the north channels, was entrenched in 1759.

No. 19, by the side of the latter is the island called *Piquet*, because this missionary took refuge there with the Indians settled at La Presentation. With a camp and artillery on this island and with the Galot islands occupied, it would not be possible to descend the river.

This post is the best to stop an enemy, if we had men enough to guard these islands. The Isle Piquet, is a league around, and cannot be landed upon except in some places that are easy to defend. They may come to it from above or below and it is well wooded.

We may go up or down on the south side of the river very conveniently. This channel was unknown until 1759. The English encamped a detachment of their army there in 1760, when they besieged Fort Lévis. There are some little islands between Isle Piquet and those already mentioned, but they are not of much consequence.

No. 20, is the *Isle à la Cuisse*, a quarter of a league in circuit, elevated in the middle, capable of holding a camp of twelve hundred men, and of being entrenched. It sweeps well, at half gun shot the north shore, and with Fort Lévis would defend the passage of the whole river. It was from these, that the enemy directed their chief attention against the fort. They placed fourteen cannon in battery and six mortars, which commanded, by more than twenty-four feet elevation, the Isle of Orakointon, on which Fort Lévis was built.

No. 21, the *Isle Magdelaine*, is a little larger than the preceding, and also commands Fort Lévis and enfilades the whole island. The enemy placed eight cannon, eight mortars and two howitzers upon it.

No. 23, *Pointe à la Corne*, would be susceptible of a good entrenchment to cover this frontier by also occupying the Isle à la Cuisse and that of Fort Lévis.

No. 22, is *Pointe à l' Yerogne,*[1] upon which was the principal camp of the English, and the head quarters of General Amherst.

Orakointon,[2] is a little low island nearly level with the water, of which Fort Lévis covered two-thirds. This fort was a redoubt of 108 toises in circuit. On the front where the landing was, there was built a horn-work of 42 toises on the outside. The landing was perfectly enfiladed by the Isle à la Magdelaine. The two larger sides were quite unequal, that on the north being the longest. They were terminated by a little flank of about five toises. Behind, it was composed of three faces like the three external sides of a hexagon.

The rampart was twenty-seven feet wide at the base, reduced to eighteen at the top, revetted with saucissons. The exterior height of the rampart was seven feet, and the interior eleven.[1]

We have added above this, wooden coffers forming a parapet nine feet wide at the base and seven high. The height within was six feet. There was a fraise between the parapet and the rampart. The ditch was five toises wide and two deep, of which one foot was under water. Upon the side of the horn-work was a ditch bordered by an oblique palisade attached to

---

[1] Point Iverogne, as written in a preceding page.— ED.

[2] Oraconenton, as elsewhere written.— ED.

[1] The accompanying steel plate engraved for this work from Mante's History, gives an accurate view of the work here described.— ED.

14

bed-pieces by wooden pins, of little strength, because they were not firmly bedded.[1]

We have built around the island on the north side, an epaulment nine feet at the base and five or six feet high, and on the N. E. point a redoubt, piece upon piece of timber eighteen inches square, pierced for five guns.

The south side, where the landing was, we had closed by a palisade up to the foot of the glacis, where were formed wooden boat slides for the use of the fort.

At the S. W. point was an epaulement as a parapet of the covered way. Around the whole island we had placed an abattis of the branches and tops of trees, which extended out fifteen feet into the water. We had left a passage to land on the north side, of forty toises, and all from the fort to the end of the island.

This fort is easily commanded by a point of land on the south side called *Ganataragoin*,[2] distant 450 toises from the island, where the enemy placed four cannon, four mortars and two howitzers, which enfiladed the island from south west to north east. On the same shore and opposite the isle of Orakointon, there is a little river[3] of the same name as that of the point we

---

[1] The whole work could only last a little while, and we believe that even in the late war, the English had abandoned it, as it was useless to them.— *Note in Original.*

[2] Now " Indian Point " in Lisbon.— ED.

[3] Tibbitt's creek in Lisbon.— ED.

have just mentioned. It has considerable width and depth for a league and a half. If a camp and a redoubt were placed there, they would very well defend the south channel of the river.

The islands we have mentioned, and Pointe à la Corne,[1] are the only posts capable of defence at the head of the rapids. The current at Point Ganataragoin is strong, and follows that shore.

The river has a good current opposite the Isle Orakointon, and forms at the lower part of the island a great eddy on the south side, which affords good ground for anchorage. Vessels could winter there very conveniently, but they would need a fresh wind from the N. E. to enable them to overcome the current, which begins at Point Ganataragoin.

Vessels can actually go down as far as in front of the Isle Piquet, but the anchorage is good for nothing, and the currents, both to the right and left, are very strong.

La Presentation, or Chouégatchie,[2] is an Iroquois establishment formed by M. l' Abbé Picquet, a Sulpician. They had there built a square fort, of which the bastions were formed by houses, and the curtains great upright timbers fifteen or sixteen feet high. The missionaries, the commandant, the little garrison and the store keeper, for the mission service estab-

---

[1] Windmill Point, on the north shore. Fort Wellington is a short distance above this fort.— ED.

[2] Oswegatchie. Now Ogdensburgh.— ED.

lished by the king, occupied the four quarters of this structure. In 1759, this mission, which was quite numerous, retired to the Isle Picquet, and the fort was dismantled so that it should not afford shelter to the enemy. The mission was very prosperous, because the lands there are excellent for tillage.

They can go very far into the country by the Chouegatchie River. The interior of this country is very little known to our Canadians, and the Indians only visit it for hunting.

There is a reef of rocks in the river almost opposite the Indian village, where the Abbé Picquet had built a saw mill. Vessels can anchor in front of the village, but they are not secure on account of the winds, and the river is subject to freshets that bring down trees.

This river has a fine navigation of twenty leagues,[1] but the remainder can only be passed in canoes with portages. It approaches the height of land, and our parties sometimes took this route in going to the English frontiers.

Back of Fort de La Presentation is a bluff very suitable to build a city or village. The location is very advantageous.[2]

The River St. Lawrence is fine, and its shores beautiful in these parts, until two leagues above Pointe

[1] That branch known as Black Lake, into which flows the Indian River, formerly much used by the natives in going by way of the Black River.— ED.

[2] The village of Ogdensburgh is laid out upon this bluff.— ED.

au Baril, as well for cultivation, as for hunting and fish which are very abundant.

The river is here not over a good quarter of a league wide, and its channel is very straight for eleven leagues from above the Galots to Toniata. It is not encumbered with islands, and it has a considerable depth of water.

At three leagues above La Presentation, on the north side, is a point of land called *Pointe au Baril*. It commands the river well, and would protect the vessels which might be stationed there to defend it. A camp might be there very advantageously placed, as a league and a half further up, the shores are steep rocks, and an enemy could not establish themselves there in force. These banks continue to the Bay of Corbeau.

Near point No. 24, is a bay called *Ance à la Construction*[1] from the vessels which were built there in 1759. It was very convenient for building, the water in front being deep and timber near. They might here make a good entrenchment to cover the workmen.

A league and a half above Pointe au Baril, is a little island marked 25, which may be 500 toises around. It is a rock upon which a fort might be built. It presents a view of the river as far as Toniata, and would sweep it very well with artillery. It has a good anchorage at the lower part. We sent the vessels to this station to observe the river.

---

[1] Probably the present site of Brockville.— ED.

From the head of this island, on the south shore, almost to the Bay of Niaoure,[1] the banks are low and full of creeks and marshy bays, and are very thickly wooded.

At five leagues from Pointe au Baril, is the Island of Toniata. The main channel of the river is between this island and the south shore. The north part of the river is filled with rushes, and in summer it is a famous eel fishery.

The Island of Toniata[2] is three leagues long by a half a quarter of a league wide. Its soil is good to cultivate, as is also true of another island situated between it and the north shore.[3] It is a league long, and a quarter of a league wide.

At the upper extremity is a little passage, with but little water,[4] and full of rushes, which they call the Petit Detroit. This is the route that bateaux always take in going up, to avoid the currents.

We should notice that we ought to pay no attention to the little channels which we meet among the rushes, and which have no outlet and would ground a vessel.

[1] Chamout Bay. — Ed.

[2] M. de Frontenac gave this island to an Iroquois, and the latter soon after sold it for four pots of brandy to a Canadian who would have in turn sold it back for a beaver skin. — *Note in Original.*

On modern maps it is *Grenadier* or *Barthurst* Island, on the Canada side of the boundary. The signification of Toniata is said to be " Beyond the Point." — Ed.

[3] Tar Island on Owen's chart. — Ed.

[4] The surroundings are here from four to six feet. — Ed.

At the Petit Detroit, they perform the ceremony of baptizing those who have never before gone up this river.

At a league and a half above, begins the Thousand Islands, which continue at least three leagues. These are an infinite number of little rocks covered with trees, which have channels quite large in some places. In others, vessels in passing through would almost touch them. They are very safe, almost always have a good depth all around, and there is but a slight current.

At the end of three leagues, we find larger islands. We should take care and not go astray. In following in bateaux the channel nearest the north side, we shall notice several inlets ending in marshes which are near the shore.

It is necessary to turn very short to enter the Bay of Corbeau,[1] which is large and fine. We pass between the south point which is very straight and a little island, which we have to pass very near. From thence they coast along the Isle au Citron which is a good league in length. It is fine and well wooded.

They make a crossing of two leagues to reach the Isle Cochois, which is three leagues long, and half a league wide, abounding in game and fish.

The view from the foot of this island, with the neighboring islands and the north shore, forms a pros-

---

[1] On Owen's chart published by the English Hydrographical office, this is named *Baumgardt Bay.* — ED.

pect most delightful on account of the beauty of the channels. This part appears to be very proper for cultivation, and good for hunting and fishing.

From thence to Fort Frontenac is three leagues. We find a bay sufficiently deep and quite good, before coming to Montreal Point, which is the south point of the Bay of Cataracoui.

Montreal Point would make an advantageous camp, being only accessible from the front, which would oblige the enemy to make a wide detour to approach it. It is a hill which slopes down to the point. [1]

Cataracoui or Frontenac,[2] is a square fort of masonry without terraces, the walls being fifteen inches thick and the outside square and forty-two toises on a side. The flanks are very small, and a wooden scaffold serves for a terre-plein. The fort is commanded on the side of the country, at a half gun-shot, and the lands in the vicinity are as curtains to one another, and so command them as to prevent this from ever being made a good post without great expense.[3]

The anchorage, which is directly opposite the fort, is

---

[1] Fort Henry is now built on this point. — ED.

[2] Cataracoui is the name of the Frontenac Bay; the latter, that of a fort built in 1672 by order of the Count Frontenac, and then abandoned but resumed in 1695, according to the intentions of this governor of New France. — *Note in Original.*

The city of Kingston now occupies the site of the fort described in the text. — ED.

[3] This post was only built to hold the Iroquois in check. — *Note in Original.*

excellent for vessels, and as winter quarters. Very near the entrance of the bay on the north side, is a cove very proper for ship building. At the head of the bay is a kind of marsh, extremely peopled by aquatic birds. The lands around have but a thin soil, yet good to till, and the interior is very fine.

This bay has the fault of not being on the lake, and it is difficult to know from there what is passing. The coast except the bay is all rock, and very difficult to land upon. It is better to seek the bay of Little Cataracoui, unless you wish to enter the large bay.

Little Cataracoui has the same entrance as the large bay, and has a depth of only a quarter of a league. The bottom is full of rushes. This former bay is of consequence, because the enemy might come and land there without being seen from Frontenac, and from thence easily come across, it being but a short league, as was executed by Bradstreet in 1758, with four thousand men, to attack this fort, which had a garrison of only fifty men, and thirty voyageurs who were there by chance.

A quarter of a league from Little Cataracoui is a large but shallow bay which they call *Sandy Bay*. It is here where they come for materials in building Frontenac.

At a league and a half farther, is another bay, formed by the mouth of a river.[1] The sides are high,

---

[1] Now Mill Creek.— ED.

and bordered by great rocks, and bateaux can not rest there in safety.

Two leagues further, in following the north shore of Frontenac we meet three little islands called *Tonégignon* [1] now deserted by the Indians. It is difficult to pass between these islands and that of Tonti, on account of large shoals that extend nearly across. We pass between the two little islands which are north and south to reach the Isle of Tonti. [2] This island is three leagues long and a league and a half wide in some places.

They follow in bateaux its north side to the end. Vessels pass to the open side of this island, in coming down, and come direct upon Little Cataracoui. There is an islet of rocks covered with trees which we must not too nearly approach on account of the shoals, especially on the upper side.

Bateaux make the traverse to the shore of the Bay of Quinte, which has an opening a league wide. They leave this bay on the right, unless they wish to make its portage, which is fifteen leagues distant at the head of the bay. This passage would enable us to avoid making the circuit of the great penisula, [3] which is not very easy. The portage is about a league, and all the way in the sand.

---

[1] The islands are called " The Brothers," on Capt. Owen's chart of the Lake.— ED.

[2] Otherwise called Amherst Island.— ED.

[3] Prince Edward's.— ED.

We follow the shore of the peninsula two leagues and a half, and then make the traverse of a bay,[1] which is three leagues wide at the mouth, and five deep. We do not know whether there is good anchorage. The north point is a rock. All this peninsula is filled with fine woods.

At a quarter of a league from the south point, it forms a narrow strait. We then pass near the Isle d' Ecoui,[2] behind which is a good anchorage. On the side of the open lake there are two banks between wind and water called *Les Gaïlans*.

The whole north shore of Lake Ontario is formed of points of from a quarter to half a league, all of which have quite large shoals, which it is difficult to double when there is but little wind. They are flat rocks.

At two leagues from the Ecouis, is a sinuosity two leagues wide and about a league deep, of which the north part is sandy, but not with sufficient depth for the anchorage of vessels. The rest is flat rock, or *galets*.

At its S. W. end is Point aux Gravois,[3] where they anchor. For two leagues the shore runs N. E. and S. W. They always coast along Point aux Gravois which is flat rock.

In the turn of this point to the S. W., and in the

---

[1] Prince Edward's Bay.— ED.

[2] Inner Drake Island.— ED.

[3] Gull Point.— ED.

west part of the first bend it has a bottom of sand, where they anchor. The second bend has a flat rock bottom.

From thence we pass to Pointe du Détour, which extends farthest into the lake.[1] Its bottom is flat rock, and it is difficult to double it when the wind is a little strong. The waves are very bad on account of the shallow bottom.

We meet near this point, some great bends of half a league in depth, and there is one before coming to the Bay of Dunes, of which the bottom for half a league is of sand, but the west side is rock, as is the case with all the other points, whose bays have a bottom of flat rock.

The Bay of Dunes,[2] is three leagues wide. The wind has there formed hills of sand as at Dunkirk, which separate the lake from a marsh[3] which is three leagues deep, and full of water fowls.

The coast of the lake as far as to the Point of Quinté,[4] is every where rock. In the eddies formed by these points are sandy bottoms where we may anchor. There are also good anchorages around the Isle of Quinté.[5] This island may be three quarters of a league across.

---

[1] Peter Point on which is now a light house.— ED.

[2] Big Sandy Bay.— ED.

[3] West Lake.— ED.

[4] Huycks or Nicholas Point.— ED.

[5] Nicholas Island.— ED.

From the Point of Quinté, we enter a bay[1] which is five leagues wide, reaching almost to Presque Isle; the shore at the head of the bay is all sand.

At about two leagues from Presque Isle, we come to the portage to the head of the Bay of Quinté. We should pass on the outside of this Presque Isle because in passing within, we get among the rushes,[2] and from thence must make a portage of three hundred paces over the sand to regain the lake.

The Presque Isle of Quinté, was an island which has been joined to the main land by the sand and gravel thrown up by the south-west winds, or washed into the bay on that side.[3] In this vicinity we find very good land. The flats up to the mountain which are not very high, are very fine meadows watered by two streams marked on the map. This country would be delightful to live in.[4] There is a great abundance of game and fish, and it is constantly frequented by the Missisake Indians.

From the Presque Isle to the River de Ganaraské,[5] the land along the shore is more suitable for cultivation than any that we find towards Frontenac. Gana-

---

[1] Weller's Bay.— ED.

[2] Now Newcastle Harbor. Brighton is a station on the Grand Trunk road, near this place.— ED.

[3] Now known as Shoal Bay. — ED.

[4] Along this shore now runs the Grand Trunk railway, with the villages of Colborne, Grafton, Coburg and Port Hope. — ED.

[5] Jones's Creek at Port Hope. — ED.

raské and Salmon River are only remarkable for being well stocked with fish.

The Petits Ecors are banks cut down forty or fifty feet, almost from a peak. They form little capes and bays at the bottom of which are the mouths of rivers or marshes, and we can only land at the bottom of the bays.

After having doubled the Petits Ecors, we come to a large bay which is two leagues wide at the opening, and the river which comes in at its head is of considerable size. Its mouth is concealed in the rushes even to the lake, which is very unusual, because almost always these mouths are gravelly, and have but a little channel leading into the lake. They here take prodigious quantities of fish, which at certain seasons go from the lake into these rivers.

At the beginning of the Grand Ecors, there appears the mouth of a considerable river.[1] These "Ecors" are banks cut down almost from a point, and eighty or a hundred feet high, and continue for five leagues.[2] At the end of this distance is a point of sand, wooded, and forming a peninsula, and in the rear a large bay partly covered with rushes. Vessels can here anchor and pass the winter.

At the point of the peninsula, there is a good anchorage, and at the bottom of the bay a river very proper for building mills, as there is fine pine timber

---

[1] River Rouge. Port Union is at its mouth. — ED.

[2] Known as the " Heights of Scarboro." — ED.

in the neighborhood. They make a portage when they go in a canoe from the bottom of this bay to the Ecors.

The fort of Toronto is at the end of the bay, upon the side which is quite elevated and covered with flat rock. Vessels cannot approach within cannon shot. This fort or post was a square of about thirty toises on a side, externally with flanks of fifteen feet. The curtains formed the buildings of the fort. It was very well built, piece upon piece, but was only useful for trade.[1]

A league west of the fort, is the mouth of the Toronto river,[2] which is of considerable size. This river communicates with Lake Huron, by a portage of fifteen leagues, and is frequented by the Indians who come from the north.

The other streams which occur towards the head of the lake, appear also of considerable size, and are advantageous chiefly for hunting and fishing.

The head of the lake forms a bar of gravel of two leagues which separates the great lake from a little one[3] which is mostly covered with rushes. At its

---

[1] The fort at Toronto was built to intercept the Indian trade from Oswego. It was first called Rouillé after the French minister of the Marine. — *Memoires sur le Canada*, 13. — ED.

[2] The River Humber. — ED.

[3] Burlington Bay. A place near the head of Burlington Bay was formerly named "Coote's Paradise," concerning which Bouchette gives the following explanatory note:

" This spot owes its name to the rhapsodic expression of an enthusiastic sportsman, who being here stationed between Burlington Bay

extremity is a river which there has a fall.   This place
is curious on account of the quantity of water fowl
that pass there, such as ducks, teals, bustards, geese
and swans.   We can shoot them very easily in their
passage of the rocks at this fall.[1]

This river goes far into the land, and communicates
with two rivers by portages, of which one falls into
Lake Erie, and the other after a course of sixty leagues,
falls into Lake St. Clair above Detroit.   This country
is very fine, and very good for hunting.   The river, of
whose name M. Pouchot has never been informed, is
without rapids, and quite navigable through its whole
course.[2]   The Indians or Canadians sent in winter
from Niagara to Detroit, went by this route, and commonly took ten days in passing from one place to the
other.   They call it a hundred leagues by this route
from Niagara to Detroit.   Several rivers occur between

and a marsh to the westward, found the sport so excellent, as the
game passed in heavy flights from the one to the other, that he digni-
fied the spot, otherwise uninteresting, with its present deluding appellation. Major Cootes belonged to the British army. — *British
Dominions in North America* (1832) i, 98.

The city of Hamilton at the head of the bay, was laid out in 1813.
In 1861 it had a population of 19,096. The Desjardins Canal affords
a navigation of four miles to Dundas. — ED.

[1] Near the present site of Dundas. — ED.

[2] There is no stream of any note that enters the lake at this point.
Grand River, a tributary of Lake Erie, rises far to the northward of
Lake Ontario, and was navigable twenty-five miles by schooners and
much farther by large bateaux. The Thames River, formerly called
Riviére à la Tranche, empties near Detroit. It is one hundred and
fifty miles long, and in a state of nature was navigable for vessels
fifteen miles, and by bateaux nearly to its source.

the head of the lake and Niagara, which is a distance[1] of fifteen leagues. They almost all issue from ranges of land which they call *cotes*, which come down to meet the river from the head of the lake. The interval between these *cotes* is a fine and well wooded plain. There are pines towards the Great Marsh and the Marsh of Three Outlets, which were used at Fort Niagara.

This kind of timber is rare in these parts, where there are usually found oak of different kinds, walnut, chesnut, and yellow wood,[2] which is very proper for building and wainscoting. They also find the black walnut — which is very fine for furniture — beech, sycamore and maple. From the latter they draw a sugar which is very good, and less corrosive than the white.

In the parts north of Toronto, we more frequently find pine and cedar, on account of its vicinity to mountains. They are not as high as the Vauges, but covered with fine timber and good soil. They are not cold like those near Carillon.

Before 1754, our voyageurs almost never in their journeys followed the north shore of the lake, where they had, however, more shelter than on the south, for a considerable number of bateaux. The route is a little longer in going to Niagara, yet they would

[1] These streams are designated: Four, Eight, Ten, Eighteen, Twenty, Thirty and Forty Mile Creeks, according to their distances from Niagara. — ED.

[2] Whitewood or tulip tree. — ED.

16

prefer now to follow this northern route, even if Oswego did not exist.

We will reserve our description of Niagara to the chapter upon the Ohio River, for the purpose of following the south shore of the lake. The coast from Niagara to the great Riviére aux Bœufs, runs east and west about twenty-four leagues. It is straight, and the bank is generally about thirty or forty feet high. The streams that we meet do not go far into the land.

The Little Marsh distant from Niagara a league and a half, is a little bay into which two or three hundred bateaux can enter. The English landed there in 1759. The rivers Aux Ecluses[1] and Deux Sorties,[2] distant five and six leagues from this place, are only noted for the pines which grow there. We see above the river Aux Bœufs[3] on the lands above the shores a little mountain which appears round, called *La Butte à Gagnon*. It is a land mark to know that we are on the lake at fifteen leagues from Niagara. When they come opposite this, the vessels bear as much as they can to the open lake so as not to pass the mouth of the Niagara River, which cannot be seen until this is passed. Vessels would be embarrassed if they could not enter it, as the N. E. winds are usually very fresh, and they could find no shelter between Niagara and the head of the lake, which would oblige them to seek

[1] Eighteen Mile Creek. — ED.

[2] Golden Hill Creek. — ED.

[3] Oak Orchard Creek. — ED.

the north shore.   In this navigation, the gales of wind from the west, and especially from the north-west, are often severe, and drive upon the south shore.

The shores form a very uniform bank along the whole course, and we find no other landmark to recognize except this hill.

The navigation from Frontenac to Niagara with vessels is usually of four, six or eight days, unless favored by a north-east wind, which usually prevails at the moon's change.   To go from Niagara to Frontenac, we are seldom out more than one night, as the winds are usually from the south-west, and are fresh.

The mouth of the Riviére aux Bœufs is a good place to land, but in coming from Niagara it is better to pass this point in the open lake, on account of a long and bad bar to the west of it.   From Niagara to this river we find few, if indeed any, shelters for bateaux in considerable number.   From this river, the shores of the lake are lower.   They turn to the south-east, and form a series of very shallow bays of about a league across.

A little before coming to Fort des Sables, we find the mouth of the River Casconchiagon,[1] which forms a bay of sufficient size and depth, but there is a bad bar at its entrance.

This river has a much longer course into the interior than any other on this coast.   It has three falls with banks on the sides almost as fine as those of Niagara.

---

[1] Genesee River.   Charlotte Landing is a village at this place. — Ed.

They enter to the head of the Baye des Sables,[1] to begin the navigation of the Casconchiagon. There is a portage of three leagues, which is the most convenient route. We will give the details of this navigation in a separate chapter so as not to interrupt our description of the lake shore.

The Fort des Sables is only some high banks of sand, which are formed around the bay of this name. It is three leagues in depth, with a good depth of water. Beyond this bay the land as far as to the foot of the Rideau des Cotes, is very low and marshy and the wood thick.

The Cayuga Bay[2] is very fine and deep. The Boucats[3] is a little bay full of little islands, or rather of great sand hills covered with wood. The shores are steep almost to the water's edge, and if this part was sounded we should probably find very good anchorages for vessels between these islands. The land adjacent is elevated and sandy, and the curtains of the shores come down near to the lake.

The lake shore is stony and strewn with rocks from this bay to Oswego, of which we shall speak in a future chapter.

The land from Oswego always sloping towards the lake is still more elevated, and the shores are usually

---

[1] Irondequoit Bay. — ED.

[2] Great Sodus Bay. — ED.

[3] Port Bay. — ED.

nothing but rocks as far as Pointe au Cabaret.[1]   This is a long point of rocks vertical from the water, from thirty to forty feet high, and forming the most advanced point.

Half a league east of Oswego is a little bay with sandy bottom, where M. de Montcalm landed and encamped when he besieged Oswego in 1756. The English have since made a clearing, and built redoubts which look upon this bay.

In this navigation we may enter with bateaux into the Riviére a la Planche — in Indian *Tensaré-Negoni*, and into that of the Grosse Ecore, or *Cassonta-Chégonar*. These rivers do not extend far into the land.

The Riviére à La Famine,[2] in Indian *Keyouanouagué*, enters very far into the interior and goes quite near to the portage of the height of land. By this route, our parties commonly went to that frontier, and along the lake and the river of the Oneidas, so as not to be discovered.

---

[1] In the present town of Scriba. — ED.

[2] Thus called since M. de la Barre, governor of Canada, lost his whole army in 1684 upon its banks by famine, in going to make war against the Iroquois. — *Note in Original.*

The army of De la Barre numbered nine hundred French and three hundred Indians that came up the St. Lawrence, and six hundred from Niagara, of whom one-third were French, making in all eighteen hundred men. Having encamped for some time on the lake shore with a swamp in the rear, many were taken sick and he returned to Frontenac and Montreal greatly reduced in numbers, and willing to sue for peace from the tribes he went to exterminate. The site of this disaster was in Jefferson County, N. Y., and the locality best answering the description is at the mouth of Sandy Creek in Ellisburgh. — ED.

From Pointe au Cabaret to the Riviére á M. le
Comte,[1] the shore forms a great semicircle of sand,
with sand hills covered with trees. Behind these are
marshy meadows as far as to the shore, and through
these the rivers wind.

Between the River Au Sables and that of La
Famine, is a little stream called in Indian *Canagatiron*.
The River Au Sables,[2] in Indian *Etcataragarenré* is
remarkable in this, that at the head of the south
branch,[3] called *Tecanonouaronesi*, is the place where the
traditions of the Iroquois fix the spot where they issued
from the ground, or rather, according to their ideas,
where they were born. Between the river Aux Sables
and that of M. de la Comte, is the little river of *Outen-
essouéta*. The river of M. de la Comte has a good
shelter for bateaux on account of an eddy of sand
formed at the mouth of the river.

They can navigate all these rivers in canoes and
their environs are good for hunting.[4]

---

[1] Stony Creek in Henderson. — ED.

[2] Sandy Creek. — ED.

[3] The source of the south branch of Sandy Creek is in swamps in
Pinckney, Lewis County, N. Y. Another fork of the south branch
heads in a swamp near the village of Copenhagen, in the town of
Denmark. — ED.

[4] There is some uncertainty as to the identity of the streams mentioned in the text. The principal streams that flow into the lake are
Nine Mile Creek, Spring Brook Creek, Catfish Creek, Butterfly Creek,
Little Salmon River, Grindstone Creek, Salmon River, Little Sandy
Creek, Sandy Creek, &c. Of these the Salmon River is much the
largest, and is probably the *Grosse Ecore* of the French. The geo-
graphy of the east end of the lake, between Stony Point and the

The Bay of Niaouré or Neyaouinré is five leagues in depth, and several streams of considerable size discharge into it. We there find good anchorage for vessels, the best being between the islands and that round peninsula[1] where M. de Montcalm came to encamp with his army before going to Oswego.

It appears that this is the best place to make an establishment on the east end of the lake. This place only connects with the main land by a bridge of gravel. The lake has so little depth that nothing can approach larger than bateaux. It would be easy to fortify, and protect vessels at anchor. The lands around the bay are admirable for cultivation, and the fishing and hunting are excellent.[2]

There are two large rivers[3] by which we can go

---

entrance of the Bay of Niaoure, (Chaumont Bay), as understood by the French, was altogether incorrect. In fact, so late as 1792, after the great purchase made by Macomb and associates, their only knowledge of the rivers of that place was derived from Sauthier's map of 1779, with manuscript additions made up at guess work, from the accounts of hunters. For example, the Black River, [La Famine] was marked as running in nearly a right line from the High Falls to the lake, and a sale was made in Paris, supposed to include six hundred thousand acres between the river and the 44° of north latitude. But upon surveying the tract, there were found but a little over two hundred thousand acres in this tract. See *Hist. Lewis Co.* — ED.

[1] Point Peninsula, on the north side of Chaumont Bay. — ED.

[2] The fisheries of Chaumont Bay have proved an item of great importance to the country. In some years the product has been estimated as high as ten thousand barrels. — ED.

[3] Black River is the only stream of any note that comes into this bay. It was a great thoroughfare for scalping parties during this war. — ED.

easily upon the routes of the English and to Oswego, and much better observe them than by going
from Frontenac. There is a good anchorage inside of the Galot Island, and all the conveniences
for a post, and to favor the navigation of the lake.
From thence we could always find ourselves ready
to go to the Oswego river whenever the occasion demanded it.

The vessels which come from the south side of the
lake and wish to enter the river, pass between the main
land and Long Island, which they call the *Chenal de la
Galette.* It is necessary to pass beyond this island to
go to Frontenac, or between the Isle à la Forêt and
the Isle Tonti.[1]

---

[1] The author makes no mention of the navigation of the channel
south of Long Island. There exists at the head of Carlton or Buck
Island the ruins of a fort partly excavated in the rock which completely commanded this channel. It was built at great expense by
the English in the revolutionary war, and might readily be made ten-
able at the present time. The ditch and
well, cut in the rock are as perfect as
when made. The history of this work is
somewhat obscure, as it was never the
scene of hostile operations, and therefore
is scarcely mentioned by historians, except as the rendezvous of scalping parties,
or as a depôt for prisoners of war. The

FORT CARLTON.

entire absence of any notice of its existence by M. Pouchot, is almost
our only authority for the statement that it was built in the revolutionary war.

This post was occupied by a British force until the commence-
ment of the war of 1812-15, when its feeble garrison of invalids was
captured without resistance by a squad of volunteers from the American shore. — ED.

The bateaux which leave Frontenac to go to Oswego, pass between the Isle à la Forêt and Long Island, instead of coasting with difficulty around by the open lake, because the waves are always high and when the wind rises there is no shelter. They cross from thence to the Isle au Chevreuil,[1] and, to the point of the Bay of Niaouré. There is a good bay in the lower part of th Isle au Chevreuil.[2]

The point of Long Island upon the lake are flat rocks or galets. All these islands are very fine to cultivate.

There is an eddy at the lower part of the Isle aux Galots near the land, where one could find a shelter in rough weather. There is a reef near the east point, which must be passed in the open lake, and then come back to the island. The anchorage for vessels is very good.

---

[1] Grenadier Island, in the lake S. W. from Cape Vincent.— ED.

[2] Basin Harbor, where the fleet of Gen. Wilkinson rendezvoused when about to descend the St. Lawrence in the fall of 1813.— ED.

CHAPTER III.

OF THE COMMUNICATION BY WAY OF THE OSWEGO RIVER TO THE ENGLISH POSSESSIONS.[1]

Oswego according to the latest construction,[2] is built upon the site where Fort Ontario stood,[3] and the English have named it the same. It is a pentagon, of which the outside is about eighty toises. It is partly of earth, revetted with saucissons on the side towards the lake. The rest is constructed of pieces of wood about three feet square. The parapets may be twelve feet thick, and the terre-plein is a platform, made of large beams fifteen inches square. The under part of these platforms, form buildings or casements. The ditch is at least five toises wide, and it

---

[1] An Itinerary published in the *N. Y. Col. Hist.*, x, 674, gives the details of this route with great minuteness.— ED.

[2] This post was at first only a trading house, which the Iroquois had allowed the English to build in 1713. It was changed to a fort in 1727, by the adroitness of the latter, who were constantly enlarging it. It having been built upon French territory, the Marquis de Beauharnois, governor of Canada, protested against this manifest usurpation.— *Note in Original.*

[3] The fort east of the river at Oswego was built in the winter of 1754-5, about 470 yards from the old one. It was 800 feet in circumference, built of logs twenty to thirty inches thick. The wall was fourteen feet high, and surrounded by a ditch fourteen feet broad and ten deep. It contained barracks for three hundred men, and was intended to mount sixteen guns.— *Gentleman's Magazine*, XXVI, 6.—ED.

has a glacis. We did not notice any out work. It was nearly finished in 1760.

The English have built around the fort, at long gun shot, four very complete block houses, one of which looks upon the side of which we have spoken, and another upon the river. This fort could be turned at cannon shot. On the side above the river, there is a kind of curtain which commands the fort, where it would be very easy to open trenches. The ground sinks down towards the fort.

The entrance of the Oswego River is narrow, on account of the rocks under water which occur in the middle. A little above, at the point of two gravelly banks, the pass is narrow and very difficult. The English have, notwithstanding this, got in vessels of twenty-two guns.

At the end of this pass are two eddies, which form as it were two ports, into which they put their bateaux as a shelter against freshets. They have even made for that which is under the fort, a jetty of wood and stone, the better to check the waters and retain them.

The rapids begin at half a league from the fort at the first bend of the river, and are very easily forded. They go up in empty bateaux by poling with four men for the large, and two for the small ones.

These large bateaux with their load, carry twenty men, and the small when empty, seven to ten. Besides these bateaux, the English have shallops such as used in whale fishing, which are very light to row, but do not amount to much for the navigation of these rivers, especially when the waters are low, when they are often obliged to get into the water to push them along, which they cannot endure.

The bottom of the river is full of little rocks which it is necessary to turn around, and in this respect it resembles the rapids of Chambly, but the river is not so wide. The land on both sides is high.

There is a foot path which follows the left of the river from the site of old Oswego, a distance of three leagues. The woods are thick, and the country abounds in knolls, and ravines proper for ambuscade.

At the end of these three leagues, the river is navigable, but at almost every league they find shallow spots where the bateaux can scarcely pass. They are then obliged to fall in line, and to pole vigorously. They get into the water, if the bateau lurches.

Above the reëmbarkation the river becomes wider, and the water quite deep. The country is level and covered with fine timber. There is quite a current at the bends, which are about a mile apart, but in the same general course. The general direction of the river is always E. N. E., and there are several islands in the channel. That, where M. de Villiers attacked Bradstreet, is five leagues above Oswego.[1]

---

[1] In 1756, a short time before Oswego was invested by the French, Col. Bradstreet had been sent thither to convey some provisions and stores. On his return he was ambuscaded on the Oswego river, by a party of French and Indians, and about seventy bateaux men were killed. The English halted on the opposite shore, and then took

Above this place the islands are more common, and we can scarcely get through among them. They are found every mile. The river at the foot of the Falls is full of islands. It is necessary to hold the north side to prevent running aground.

They land at a long gun shot from the portage, and send up the bateaux by poling in the current to the foot of the Falls, where they have a road made with round pieces of wood to draw up the bateaux. At a hundred paces above the Falls the water is of good depth.

The English have built at this portage[1] a star fort, of timbers fifteen feet high, and a foot in diameter. This fort is commanded on the N. E. at half gun shot. It might hold a hundred or a hundred and fifty men. They have here built some store houses for the storage of goods.

The river above the portage is fine and wide, like the Sorel, and with but little current. The bends are from a quarter to half a league apart. There are three shallows at the forks of the Seneca and Oswego

---

possession of a small island where the river could be forded, and soon after attacked a part of the enemy that had already crossed, and routed them with much loss, as he also did another part that crossed at another place. The French had about a hundred killed and seventy taken prisoners. The chief loss of the English occurred among the bateaux-men at the beginning of the attack. The next morning Bradstreet was largely reinforced, but the French had disappeared, having returned to their vessels, or to the camp at the east end of the lake where they were preparing for a descent upon Oswego. — *Mante*, 61 ; *Entick*, i, 471.— ED.

[1] Now the village of Fulton, Oswego Co., N. Y.— ED.

River.[1] That which is half a league from the confluence is the largest.

It is to be observed, that the whole river has but
little depth, and the bottom is full of flat stones
covered with a very slippery mud, which obliges them
to iron the poles and oars used in this navigation.

The River of the Five Nations, or the Seneca River,
is fine, and a little larger than the Oswego, its depth
is good, and the navigation is reliable to the end.
This river communicates with many lakes, and with
the different Iroquois nations, as we see by the map.
The land in the vicinity is very fine, and full of beautiful timber.

We find at the confluence, a fort of four bastions of
about forty toises on the outside, made piece upon
piece. There are three large store houses in this fort.
It is located on the east side of the river. The
country around is very flat.

At three leagues above this confluence, there are
two shallows which are not very difficult. Three
quarters of a league before coming to the Oneida Lake,
there is a bar of flat rock, which leaves only a passage
in the middle of the river. It is necessary in passing
to get into the water waist deep. The English have
thrown great trees across the river to turn the water

---

[1] The junction of the Oneida and Seneca rivers, is since known as
Three River Point, in the present town of Clay, Onondaga Co. In
the early years of settlement, and when the natural navigation of the
country was principally used by the emigrants, it was an important
point, but it has long since ceased to be of any consequence.— Ed.

into this passage, which is the worst shallow in the river.[1]

At the entrance of the lake there occurs still another shoal, but it can be easily passed with a little care. There is a fort at the entrance of the lake, which serves as an entrepôt. It is entrenched by earth revetted with saucissons, poorly fraised, and with a ditch a dozen paces wide.[2]

The English had built two large flat bateaux, to transport across this lake. The New Jersey militia, on their return from Canada in 1760, having crowded upon one of these boats to be carried across, were taken by a gale of wind upon this lake, which is sometimes very rough on account of its shallow water. The boat was stove, and more than two hundred persons perished.

The Oneida Lake[3] is eight leagues long, two and a half leagues wide at the widest part, and on an average a league to a league and a half. The two sides appear to have no banks, and the country is low and bordered with rushes.

The Indians only navigate this lake with elm bark canoes. It freezes every winter, and breaks up in March, when the moon is full. The ice does not go

[1] The Oneida River forms now a part of the canal system of the state of New York. It has two steamboat locks 120 by 30 feet, and of three and three and a half feet lift.— ED.

[2] Fort Brewerton.— ED.

[3] This lake is 141 feet above Lake Ontario.— ED.

out, which hinders the navigation a little. We see above this lake at three or four leagues to the right, some mountains which are quite high but rounded. They are the Cayuga mountains.[1]

There is a sand bar at the mouth of Wood Creek, where a bateau never passes without touching, and to get over it is necessary to go straight towards the fort, and then turn into the river holding more to the right than the left.

Upon the west shore the English have built a large redoubt[2] all covered with the woods, piece upon piece, and above this there is built an ancient work. This is a grand entrepôt of every thing that passes on this river.

The boats come to load in the first bend of the river, where there are built some great magazines for storage. This fort is situated on a peninsula formed by the bend of the river.

At the end of the lake on the west is a river[3] upon which the Oneida village is located, upon that which is found near the end of the side where we enter the lake, occur the Onondaga villages. That called *Cassonncta* was formerly ravaged by M. de Vaudreuil.[4] It

---

[1] The high lands in Madison Co., now have no particular name.—ED.

[2] The site of this fort is now occupied by the bed of Wood Creek.—ED.

[3] Oneida Creek.—ED.

[4] The first of this family who had been governor of Canada, and whose numerous descendants have not ceased to render signal services to the state. — *Note in Original.*

Details of this expedition are given in *N. Y. Col. Hist.*, ix, 651, *et seq.* — ED.

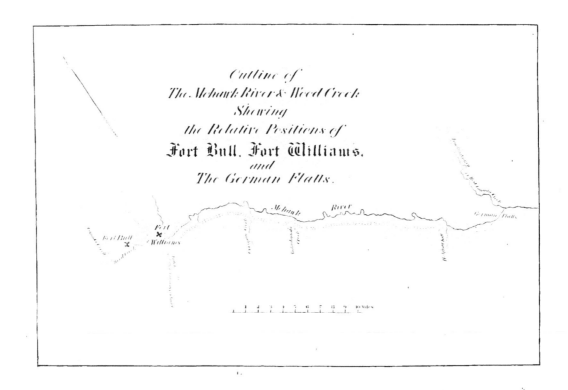

Outline of
The Mohawk River & Wood Creek
Shewing
the Relative Positions of
Fort Bull, Fort Williams,
and
The German Flatts.

was then upon the banks of a brook, and it is the village from whence they drew their name of Onondagas.

The river, called Wood Creek, is only thirty toises wide at its mouth, and the water is very dark, and not good to drink. The stream is very winding, and deep enough for four or five leagues, with very little current, and a bottom of sand and mire.

The bends are not more than a gunshot apart, and the further up we go, the shorter they become. The river is so narrow that a tree would reach across it, and they could cross it in this manner. In 1756, the English made in this way an abatis a mile in length, to cover themselves from the French, who had taken Oswego. The trees were cleared out with great difficulty, although they had only to open them so as to pass bateaux in single file, when they would almost touch on both sides, and had to often drag in the mire for want of water.

The river is the most suitable place to cut the English communication with the lakes, by abatis, which they could make to close the channel of the river. A land road would be very long and difficult to make, because the country is intersected by marshy bottom lands.

At three leagues from the source of Wood Creek, there is a little fort of upright timbers, to cover the sluices which they have built to hold the water, and to favor the passage of loaded bateaux. While they are retaining the water, they are obliged to get into

18

the stream, and drag the bateaux along over the gravel, where there is sometimes not more than six inches of water.

These sluices are not so well guarded but that they might be broken at the same time that the abatis was made. When we come to the summit of the land, the country is full of swamps and the woods thick and covered with pines.

Several rivers which flow in different directions, take their rise in these elevated lands. A quarter of a league from this, begins the river Des Agniers or the Mohawk, which is larger and much deeper than the preceding. Its least straits are knee deep even near its source. The lands adjacent are good to cultivate.

Fort Stanwix is built at a gun shot from the river, upon a slope of land which falls towards the river bank. The slope at the fort is slight. We observe this, because the surface in coming from the woods into the clearing commands the fort a very little.

This fort is a square of about ninety toises on the outside, and is built of earth, revetted within and without by great timbers, in the same fashion as that of Oswego.

In September, 1760, it was not entirely finished. It is the grand entrepôt of the English for all that passes from their colonies to the lakes, and where they usually assemble their armies, and all the bateaux employed in the navigation of these countries.

They are obliged to make the portage of half a

league upon drays to change rivers. Those drays have
two pairs of wheels, very light, joined together by a
reach, proportioned in length to the bateaux. They
can be loaded by eight men and even less. They place
the forward end of the bateau upon the forward axle,
and then the hind end. Two ordinary horses can draw
this wagon very easily at a good trot. We may judge
from this, of the lightness of these bateaux, which are
made of pine, and can carry twenty-five men; yet they
scarcely last through a campaign. The English always
keep wagons at this fort for making the portage.

From this post the river is nearly as wide as the
Seine at Paris. It has an even and sufficiently strong
current along its whole course. Its bends may be
from a quarter to half a league long. It flows through
a level and beautiful country for eighteen or twenty
leagues. Some shoals are met at the bends, but they
are not very bad. There are also some trees which
hinder somewhat the navigation, if care is not taken.
The banks of the river are sufficiently high and the
soil good.

The English have built a little fort of timbers at
about half way between the settlements and Fort
Stanwix to place their convoy, and where they could
take shelter from our parties. It is of no account, and
they call it *Schüller*.[1]

At four or five leagues above the settlements that

---

[1] Fort Schuyler, on the site of the modern city of Utica. — Ed.

have been abandoned, we begin to see ranges of little
mountains running east and west, about half a league
apart, which come down to the river and form shoals.
The first settlements we meet, are ten or twelve houses
destroyed by M. Belestre's party.[1]

The right of the river is covered by Fort Harkmar,
which will hold two hundred men, and where there is
always a garrison. This is a star redoubt of earth,
revetted with saucissons, and with a ditch fifteen or
eighteen feet wide, palisaded at the bottom and upon
the berm outside; with three or four poor cannon bearing upon the river.

It is a gun shot from a hill high enough to command
it.

The valley is here not over a mile wide, and the
houses have not an air of affluence. Opposite the fort,
is the mouth of a river,[2] which comes down from very
far among the mountains. It is quite rapid at its
mouth, where it forms a shoal, which compels the
bateaux, great and small, to come close under the fort.

---

[1] In November, 1757, M. de Belestre with 300 men, Canadian Ma-
rines and Indians, approached the Mohawk settlements by way of the
Black River, and attacked the fort at German Flats, on the south side
of the Mohawk opposite the mouth of West Canada Creek, which
surrendered without resistance. Five other small forts also surrendered at discretion. Sixty houses with barns and a mill were
burned, forty of the settlers were killed and a hundred and fifty taken
prisoners, and a large number of cattle and a vast amount of property
destroyed. All this damage was done within forty-eight hours, and
the party returned laden with plunder. — *Benton's Herkimer Co.*, p.
51. — ED.

[2] West Canada Creek. — ED.

The settlements in this quarter are too far apart to protect one another.

From this fort for a space of two leagues, the river has quite a strong current with shoals at every bend, that are quite difficult to pass. They are easy to upset upon, which occasions much injury to the freight.

The chain of little mountains becomes higher at this part, and we enter a kind of gorge of which the sides are detached rocks, mingled with a poor growth of timber.[1]

At two miles below the Falls, the English have a station where they keep wagons to transport goods and bateaux. The road of the portage is in this gorge between the rocks upon marshy ground, which is covered with round sticks of wood.

The river flows a full mile between these rocks, and forms at the bottom a little fall, at the foot of which they very easily embark. The rock of this fall is not very high, and the water at its foot is very still. It forms a very fine basin between high cliffs, that rise vertical from the water, and are crowned with woods. The basin may extend three hundred toises before coming out from these rocks.

This is the best post that could be found on this route, and a few people stationed upon these rocks would be able to stop quite an army. This place appears to have been made for a natural boundary.

[1] Little Falls. — ED.

The landscape here changes entirely, as well as the nature of the soil. In coming out of this mountain the country widens, and the valley is about a league across. The soil is very fine and well cultivated, the dwellings better built and about a quarter of a league apart along the river, in the fields and among the hills.

This country is shut in like the preceding by little mountains, which have an east and west course. They come down to the river and form shoals and little rapids more frequently than in the upper part of this river, where it is not inhabited.

The river makes quite a curve in the place called *Conyoxery*,[1] where we find a little stream that comes from the mountains, and winds across the fields about as wide as a large ditch. The Mohawk maintains in its course a considerable width, and a rapid current, excepting upon the shoals that we meet at almost every league. There is another river quite large near the first Mohawk village, which comes from the west. It does not appear to be navigable, and its course is not so long.[2]

There is here an old and miserable wooden fort, upon the bank, and at the confluence of the two rivers. We find some English dwellings in this village, mingled with those of the Indians.

At two leagues below is the great village of the

---

[1] Canajoharie. — Ed.

[2] Nowadaga Creek. — Ed.

Mohawks, where there is quite a large fort built piece upon piece, called *Fort Hunter*.[1] It is built upon quite a large river which winds past the fort. It comes from the mountains behind the sources of the Delaware.[2] These two villages may have a hundred and fifty or two hundred warriors. These Indians are the most devoted to the English, and they are of the protestant religion.

From this village the mountains begin to close up, and at a league below there is only a kind of gorge, but it is still inhabited on the slopes of the hills. The house of Colonel Johnson, who is charged with everything relating to Indian affairs, is in this gorge, at two leagues below the second Indian village.[3] It is at the head of a little flat of lawn, which extends to the banks of the river. Upon the right side of the house is a little stream, coming from the hills and very shallow. This house is a kind of chateau, with a projection in front, and crowned by a curb roof. It has quite a large front yard, with a wall around it, and two turrets of some height on each side of the entrance

---

[1] This was a short distance east of Schoharie Creek, and adjacent to the Mohawk. The Erie Canal passes directly over its site. — Ed.

[2] Schoharie Creek. — Ed.

[3] This house is still standing in Amsterdam, three miles west of the village and near the N. Y. C. R. R. It was built about 1740, and was the home of Sir William Johnson until about 1761-2, when he removed to near the present village of Johnstown. The stream that comes down by the side of the mansion noticed in the text, is the Kayaderoseros. The place was often mentioned as "Fort Johnson" or "Mount Johnson," and is now owned by A. Young, Esq. Compare description given in *N. Y. Col. Hist.*, x, 679. — Ed.

gate on the side of the lawn. The rear of the house
is set in between two swells of the mountains. Upon
the one on the right is a blockhouse to somewhat cover
the chateau, but is itself commanded by the hills at
pistol shot. This house is isolated, and very open to
an attack. If they had known this, our parties might
have very easily carried off Colonel Johnson. Almost
opposite his house in the hills on the other side, is a
road that goes down the valley of the Susquehanna.

The river from this place, flows always in a deep
channel, and the bends vary from less than a gun shot
to a quarter of a league or more in length. In all
these checks of the current there are shoals and bars
difficult to pass, and the land along here is not good.

At a league from Schenectady, or Corlack, the
country opens wide, and presents more of an elevated
plain scattered with hills, but without mountains.
The prospect is fine, and the land appears fertile.

The river as far as Schenectady has little water, and
has frequent shoals. In front of this place is an island,
in a very large meadow, formed by the Mohawk and
another river, which almost surrounds the city.

Schenectady is well built, the streets well laid out,
and the houses in the Flemish style. It may contain
three thousand souls.[1] Its position would be admira-

---

[1] This must be an over estimate. In the itinerary above quoted, it
is mentioned as a village of three hundred houses. And is thus described:

"It is surrounded by upright pickets, flanked from distance to distance. Entering this village by the gate, on the Fort Hunter side,

ble, were it not for a hill in front of the Orange gate, at short musket range.

There is found quite a rugged rise of ground in coming out of the suburbs. The remainder of the circuit of the city is a peninsula, raised upon a terrace of land some forty feet high. A stream that is not fordable extends around every side except that towards Orange. Upon the banks of this river are some very fine gardens.

The city is only surrounded by cedar posts without flanks, and could not be defended against a large party.

They do not navigate the river between Schenectady and the Falls. It is extremely broken through this whole distance. From Schenectady to Albany it is five leagues, entirely by land, and the country is rough and desert. We only find two or three inns at midway.

These hills are sand dunes, covered with pines. The land descends to Albany.

At Schenectady they made all bateaux used by the armies that went upon Lake Ontario. If they had taken them from Albany, they would need to be carried upon trucks to Schenectady.

---

there is a fort to the right which forms a species of citadel in the interior of the village itself. It is a square, flanked with four bastions or demi-bastions, and is constructed half of masonry, and half of timbers piled one over the other above the masonry. It is capable of holding two or three hundred men. There are some pieces of cannon in battery on the ramparts. It is not encircled by a ditch. The entrance is through a large swing gate with lifts up like a draw bridge.— *N. Y. Col. Hist.*, x, 677.— ED.

19

CHAPTER IV.

OF THE COMMUNICATION FROM LAKE ONTARIO TO THE
ENGLISH FRONTIERS BY WAY OF THE CASCONCHIAGON.

The Bay of Casconchiagon, as we have formerly
said, would be very good for the anchorage of vessels,
but its entrance is difficult on account of a bar. If
the country were inhabited, we might still make a
very convenient passage.

They usually pass into the Bay of Fort des Sables,
to go to make the portage from its head, and from
thence go up the banks, to enter this river.

At present this navigation is only made in bark
canoes. It would be necessary to have bateaux in
reserve above the falls,[1] where the water is deep
enough, and the currents gentle for the navigation of
bateaux. This river has no portages but those marked
on the map. It traverses the whole country of the
Five Nations, and communicates with the Ohio by a
little lake, the waters of which in part fall into the
Casconchiagon, and in part into the Ohio. It is
doubtless one of the most elevated points in America,

---

[1] These are three in number; the first sixty feet high and two arpents wide, the third a hundred feet high and three arpents wide.
The second is much less considerable. Journ. du P. Charlevoix, tom.
v., p. 330.— *Note in Original.*

since its waters divide, a part flowing into the Gulf of St. Lawrence, and a part into the Gulf of Mexico. There is near this lake a bitumenous oil spring of considerable size.[1]

The multitude of lakes, the facility of navigation, and the few portages, all indicate that these are very elevated plains, and indeed we do not meet with great mountains, except in proportion as we go from the sources of these rivers.

The navigation of this river would be much more considerable, if these countries should come to be inhabited by Europeans. One of its branches as we have seen, communicates with the Ohio, and another with the Canestio, by a portage of a league. The latter joins the Susquehanna, of which it is one of the branches.

The banks of the Casconchiagon,[2] and of the Canestio, are the parts chiefly inhabited by the Senecas, who are the most numerous of the Five Nations. The whole country along these rivers is beautiful and fertile, as is also in general the whole the Iroquois inhabit. Their villages are near the lakes, where we find meadows forming landscapes of the most charming kind, and lands which would be most admirable

---

[1] According to the account of M. de Joncaire, there are two of these fountains. The Indians use their waters to soothe all kinds of pain. Journ. cit. p. 331.—*Note in Original.*

[2] Extending a hundred leagues, according to Father Charlevoix. Journ. cit., p. 330. — *Ib.*

to cultivate.   It is in the country of the Five Nations that we most frequently find the plant called *gin-seng*.[1]

The Iroquois nation which comprehends six nations, may have about two thousand warriors, according to the rank they hold among themselves, namely:

The Onondagas,	300
The Senecas,	700
The Cayugas,	350
The Oneidas,	250
The Agniers or Mohawks,	150
The Tuscaroras,	100

[1] We owe the discovery of this plant to Father Lafitau. This missionary was convinced that he could find it in Canada, and after a very long search he found it in this country.   He saw with much surprise, that the Chinese word *gin-seng*, signifying "resembling a man," or as the translator of P. Kircher renders it "a man's thigh," and that the Iroquois word *garent-oguen*, had the same meaning; *orenta*, in Iroquois signifying the "thighs," and the "legs," and *oguen*, expresses "two things separated." He published this discovery in 1718, in a pamphlet dedicated to his Highness the Regent, and to flatter this prince, called this plant *Aureliana Canadensis, sinesibus gin-seng, Iroquois, garentoguen*. M. Sarrasin, a physician of Quebec, had in 1704, sent some of these plants to the king's garden, but they then knew nothing about it in Paris. It is found in many countries of North America, which are on about the same parallel as Corée, from whence comes the most that the Chinese use.   Gin-seng is as common in the Illinois country, as with the Iroquois. It also occurs in Maryland, &c.   As soon as it was proved that the *garentoguen* was the *gin-seng*, they hastened to collect it. The India company paid the Canadians as high as 96 livres the pound, to take to China. It then fell to four livres, and finally into discredit entirely, from reasons given by the Abbé Raynal, in his *Hist. Phil. & Pol. des Etab. des Européens*, &c. — *Note in Original. Memoires sur le Canada*, 27. — *Raynal's Hist. des Indies*, vi, 150.

This plant is the *Panax quinquefolia* of botanists. It is still an article of trade with China, but of very uncertain price. Its medicinal virtues have been altogether over rated. — ED.

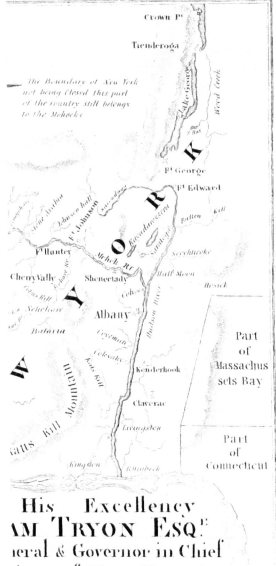

Crown P^t

Tienderoga

*The Boundary of New York
not being Closed this part
of the country still belongs
to the Mohocks*

Y O R K

F^t George

F^t Edward

F^t Johnson

Kayaderusseria

F^t Hunter   Mohck R^r

CherryVally   Shenectady

Albany

Batavia   Kenderhook

Claverac

Livingston

Kingston   Rhinbeck

Part
of
Massachus
sets Bay

Part
of
Connecticut

His   Excellency

AM TRYON ESQ^r

neral & Governor in Chief

vince of NEW-YORK & &

This Map

ntry of the VI. Nations

Part of the Adjacent Colonie,

cribed by his Excellency's

Most Obedient humble Servant

Guy Johnson   1771

to cultivate.   It is in the country of the Five Nations
that we most frequently find the plant called *gin-seng*.[1]

The Iroquois nation which comprehends six nations,
may have about two thousand warriors, according to
the rank they hold among themselves, namely :

The Onondagas,................................ 300
The Senecas,................................... 700
The Cayugas,.................................. 350
The Oneidas,.................................. 250
The Agniers or Mohawks,................. 150
The Tuscaroras,.............................. 100

---

[1] We owe the discovery of this plant to Father Lafitau. This missionary was convinced that he could find it in Canada, and after a
very long search he found it in this country. He saw with much surprise, that the Chinese word *gin-seng*, signifying " resembling a man,"
or as the translator of P. Kircher renders it " a man's thigh," and that
the Iroquois word *garent-oguen*, had the same meaning; *orenta*, in
Iroquois signifying the " thighs," and the " legs," and *oguen*, expresses
" two things separated." He published this discovery in 1718, in a
pamphlet dedicated to his Highness the Regent, and to flatter this
prince, called this plant *Aureliana Canadensis, sinensibus gin-seng,
Iroquois, garentoguen*. M. Sarrasin, a physician of Quebec, had in
1704, sent some of these plants to the king's garden, but they then
knew nothing about it in Paris. It is found in many countries of
North America, which are on about the same parallel as Corée, from
whence comes the most that the Chinese use. Gin-seng is as common
in the Illinois country, as with the Iroquois. It also occurs in Maryland, &c. As soon as it was proved that the *garentoguen* was the *gin-
seng*, they hastened to collect it. The India company paid the
Canadians as high as 96 livres the pound, to take to China. It then
fell to four livres, and finally into discredit entirely, from reasons
given by the Abbé Raynal, in his *Hist. Phil. & Pol. des Etab. des
Européens*, &c. — *Note in Original. Memoires sur le Canada*, 27. —
Raynal's Hist. des Indies, vi, 150.

This plant is the *Panax quinquefolia* of botanists. It is still an
article of trade with China, but of very uncertain price. Its medicinal
virtues have been altogether over rated. — ED.

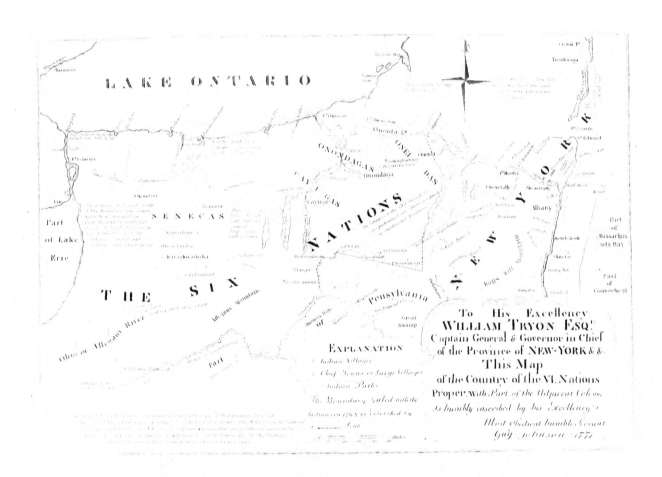

LAKE ONTARIO

NEW YORK

ONONDAGAS

ONEIDAS

CAYUGAS

SENECAS

THE SIX

NATIONS

Part of Lake Erie

Ohio or Alleghany River

Allegany Mountain

Pensylvania

Great Swamp

Part

Part of Massachusetts Bay

Part of Connecticut

Albany

EXPLANATION

Indian Villages

Chief Towns or Large Villages

Indian Paths

The Boundary settled with the Indians in 1768 is described by a ———— line

To His Excellency
WILLIAM TRYON Esq.
Captain General & Governor in Chief
of the Province of NEW-YORK &c &c.
This Map
of the Country of the VI. Nations
Proper, with Part of the Adjacent Colonies,
Is humbly inscribed by his Excellency's
Most Obedient humble Servant
Guy Johnson 1771

SOUTH EAST VIEW OF THE GREAT CATARACT
ON THE STOCKBRIDGE OR LITTLE SENECA RIVER, LAKE ONTARIO.

We may judge from this statement, the population of this nation. Can we believe that they have been much enfeebled from intercourse with Europeans?[1] Our historians are unwarranted in saying that armies of ten and twenty thousand men have marched to subjugate some one or other of the American nations. Within this time, we have had no knowledge of any particular plague that has destroyed them.[2] They may therefore have exaggerated in their accounts.[3]

The banks of the Canestio River are also inhabited by the Abenakis. We call them *Loups,* and the English *Mohaigans.* There is also a village of the Foxes, or Outugamis, who have fled thither since the last war that this nation had with the French.

The Loups who inhabit the valleys of the Susquehanna, may put from fifteen to eighteen warriors on foot. The village of Theaogen alone has six hundred. The little village of Tateyonons, which furnishes but sixty warriors, is allied with the Iroquois.

The Susquehanna River is navigable almost from its source. It flows through a beautiful valley filled with very fine timber. Along its course it has a very good depth of water to carry bateaux as far as to Fort Shamokin.

---

[1] There can be no doubt but that the Indian nations have diminished greatly during this period. See the end of this work. — *Note in Original.*

[2] May not the small pox and brandy be regarded as two great curses to all the Indians of this continent? — *Ib.*

[3] This may be, but the diminution although not as great, is not the less as certain. — *Ib.*

The west branch of this river is rather a torrent than a river. As it is buried among rude mountains, it is very rapid. The Indians, however, go down in their canoes at high water.

From Shamokin to the Chesapeake Bay, the Susquehanna has rapids which are met with at the chains of mountains which run east and west throughout the English possessions. The worst of these is that of Canowega. These rapids prevent the English from using this river much for the interior navigation of their possessions.

From Fort Shamokin the navigation is the easiest they have, to go to the Five Nations and upon the lakes. But the interposition of the Loup and Iroquois Indians, has hitherto prevented them from forming establishments in that quarter.

Before the last war they had pressed up as far as near Theaogen, which the Indians made them abandon, and as far up as below the Juniata valley, which is beautiful and fertile. But they were obliged ro retire from this also.[1]

---

[1] The English have returned in force since the time when M. Pouchot wrote, to the banks of the Ohio and its tributaries, and have compelled the Indians to let them alone. A few years before the actual war, the court at London formed a project to send a powerful colony into that country. The celebrated economist Young, wrote against this project, which the troubles in America prevented them from carrying into effect. — *Note in Original.*

CHAPTER V.

OF THE COMMUNICATION FROM NIAGARA TO THE BELLE-
RIVIERE OR OHIO—IN ENGLISH ALLIGENY; AND FROM
THE OHIO IN PENNSYLVANIA AND VIRGINIA.

Fort Niagara is situated at the east point of the
river of this name, which is still only the St. Lawrence.[1]
A triangle terminates this point, whose base is at the
head of a horn-work of a hundred and fourteen toises
on the outside, built of earth, turfed within and without, with a ditch eleven toises wide and nine deep. It
has a demi-lune and two little lunettes, or entrenched
strongholds, with a covered way and glacis proportioned to the works. The ditches are not revetted.

The stronghold and the demi-lune are palisaded upon
the berm. The other two sides have a simple
entrenchment also of earth sodded within and without, seven feet high on the inside, and six feet thick at
the top of the parapet, with a fraise upon the berm.
These two sides of the entrenchments are upon a steep
bank forty feet high. The part towards the river

---

[1] This river is properly only an outlet of the great lakes into the sea,
and the Niagara River, from Lake Erie into Lake Ontario. It is therefore useless to seek the sources of this great river in the countries
situated to the north or north-west of Lake Superior. — *Note in Original.*

would be accessible but with difficulty. That towards the lake is steeper. There are no stones found around Niagara, and they are brought from the foot of the Cotes, or Platon.[1] There are there found large detached blocks of sandstone very proper for all kinds of masonry, but we do not find good stone for cutting. Before 1759, we were always obliged to bring lime for the use of the fort, from Frontenac, but M. Pouchot, commandant at Niagara, found some very good limestone at the head of the Cotes. We doubt whether the English know it, for they are obliged to bring lime from Oswego. They could build a city with these blocks.

There is a bar in front of the fort, which lies a good quarter of a league into the lake, and nothing can pass over it but bateaux.

The entrance of the river is difficult when they do not know where to find it, on account of the bar, and a considerable current from the river, which throws us into the eddies, and may cast us upon the bar. This passage is well defended by artillery at the point of the fort, because vessels can only ascend against this current with difficulty, and then find themselves under the batteries of the fort. They are even obliged sometimes to throw a line ashore, to haul themselves up to the anchorage, which is a tablet of sand below the middle of the fort. Vessels anchored there can

---

[1] The present site of Lewiston.— Ed.

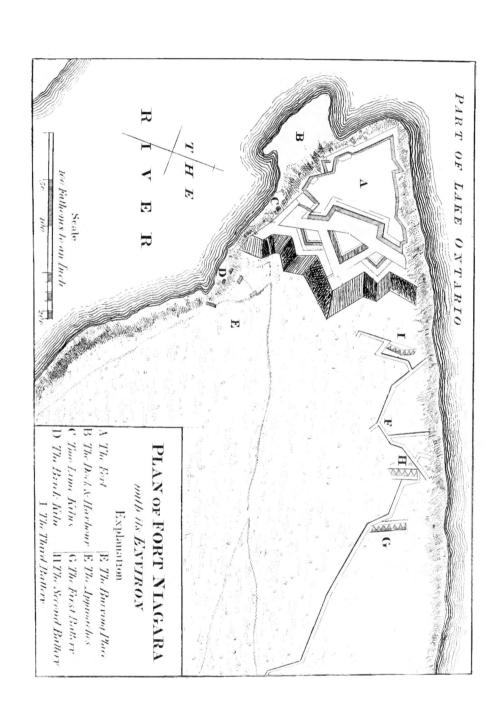

PART OF LAKE ONTARIO

THE RIVER

Scale
100 fathoms to an Inch

Scale numbers: 50 100 200

A
B
C
D
E
I
F
H
G

PLAN of FORT NIAGARA
with its ENVIRON

Explanation

A The Fort
B The Dock & Harbour
C Two Lime Kilns
D The Brick-kiln

E The Burying Place
F The Approaches
G The First Battery
H The Second Battery
I The Third Battery

touch the shore, and there is notwithstanding sufficient depth for a man-of-war.[1]

The passage by way of the Niagara, is the most
frequented on the continent of America, because this
tongue of land communicates with three great lakes,
and the navigation leads all the Indians to pass this
place, wherever they may wish to go. Niagara is
therefore the centre of trade between the Indians and
Europeans, and great numbers come thither of their
own accord from all parts of the continent.

Vessels cannot winter in the Niagara River, because
they are continually cut by the ice coming from Lake
Erie, from the month of December to the beginning
of March. There might, however, be made a port of
shelter on the west side at Mascoutin Point.[2]

The river from its mouth, to a distance of three
leagues above, to the place named *Le Platon*, has a
channel about four hundred toises wide; the current

---

[1] We present two maps of Fort Niagara. The larger one is from
Pouchot's Memoirs, with the addition of the last parallel of the English on the lake shore, at the siege of 1759. The other, from an English authority represents all the approaches of the siege.

The present fort occupies the same site, and very nearly the same
area as originally. It is one mile distant from the modern village of
Youngstown. There is a light house at the mouth of the Niagara.
On the Canada side, is the present town of Niagara, formerly Fort
George, and originally Newark. It was once the seat of government
of Upper Canada. It is in the county of Lincoln and by the last
census, the town and village had a population of 4,470. Fort Mississauga is a strong work on the Canada side opposite Fort Niagara.—
ED.

[2] Now Mississauga Point. Fort Mississauga now defends the British side of the river near this place.— ED.

20

is gentle, and it has a depth sufficient to bear a frigate as far as to the Platon, and to anchor any where along this distance. It has three bends in this course, each of a league, which gives a fine view to Niagara. The river flows for three leagues between two rocks, almost perpendicular and two or three hundred toises high, with such great force that it cannot be navigated between the Platon, and the basin under the falls.

Half a league above the falls, the river which is about half a league wide, has only a strong current. It from thence descends in boiling waves to the falls, where it plunges vertically a hundred and forty feet, upon a bank of very hard rocks. Its breadth is about nine hundred toises. The rest of this waterfall makes a very open arc, at two thirds of which we see a little wooded island which looks as if it was even ready to be engulphed.[1]

At the bottom of the falls, the river forms a great basin between the rocks, where the water is so still that they can cross it in bateaux. From the foot of the fall, the waters rebound nearly forty feet high, which makes them appear like ice.

We often find on the shores of this basin, fish,

---

[1] Father Charlevoix assures us that this island is quite narrow, and an eighth of a league in length. He adds that there are many rocks scattered here and there, from the shore and above, considerably checking the upper current. We see similar rocks covered with wood at the falls of the Rhine at Lauffen.— *Note in Original.*

The island which divides the falls, is now called Goat Island. A bridge connects it with the American shore.—ED.

bears, deer, geese, ducks and various kinds of birds which have been killed in passing over, having been drawn in by the water, or the current of air formed by the falls. The Indians collect these.

There is a wagon road from Fort Niagara to the Platon, but they generally go by water in summer. In winter they are always obliged to go by land, on account of the ice. The road from Platon to the fort at the portage,[1] is about three leagues, which they travel in three hours. As it passes through the woods, it is sometimes muddy. If it were properly drained it would be very fine.

They have at the bottom of the banks on the Platon, three large buildings to serve as an entrepôt for goods that are being transported. The shore where they land is at least sixty feet high, and is very difficult, for they have never built any thing to accommodate the landing.

The banks are three curtains, whose height from the Platon to above the banks, is equal to that of Mendon, and not steeper. There are two roads for going up; one for wagons, which is a quarter of a league longer. It has two very moderate slopes. The

---

[1] The fort at the portage was subsequently commanded by John Joseph Schlosser a German officer in the 60th Regiment, English, and was subsequently known at "Fort Schlosser." There is now a steamboat landing near this spot, which is at the foot of navigation on the Niagara River. The steamboat Caroline, was moored here when attacked by a party from Canada, cut loose, fired and sent over the falls, on the night of December 29, 1837.— Ed.

other is a foot path, which comes directly down the banks. This is very steep, and travelers and others who carry packs, always pass that way. They never stop to rest, although it takes half an hour to get up. There is a building for storage at the top of the banks.

The memoir of M. Belin represents this place as if it were one of the most difficult passes of the Alps, although above and below these banks there are large plains.

The fort at the foot of the portage, is only an enclosure of upright posts. They had there built some buildings for goods in transit, and for the service of the fort. It is here that they embark for Lake Erie. From this place, the river is not navigable more than a quarter of a league, and it is still necessary to be cautious not to be drawn into the current of the falls. The land around this fort is level and very good. This place is capable of having such a work as is needed.

On the west side of the river, at the height of this fort, is a fine little river called *Chenondac*,[1] whose banks bear very fine timber, which is procured for building the bateaux used in this navigation, as well as boards and plank for the use of the fort.

It requires care to get in and out of the Chenondac. After going a league above to cross, they descend

---

[1] Chippewa Creek.— ED.

along the bank to its mouth, and likewise in returning they have to go up the river and descend upon the fort, passing between the islands which are found in the river above it.

The river is full of islands in its channel, up to near the little rapid, as we can see by the map. The current is gentle, and they navigate by oars or sails. Some of these islands are handsome meadows.

On the east side, at three leagues from the foot of the portage, is the Riviére aux Bois Blancs.[1] This is the stream by which the Five Nations come down to the river. Its current is very slow, and in several places the land is cultivated by the Indians. The lands in the environs are very fine. This river is full of fish.

The Little Rapid is the outlet of Lake Erie. It is a reef, where the current is smooth but strong, for half a league.[2] The river is a good quarter of a league wide, and has a rock bottom. Its depth not great, yet we find passages, where if the vessels were properly constructed, they could go up with a good wind. The bateaux ascend by poling or towing.

The eastern shores of the lake are higher than those on the west, and both appear to be very good.

Lake Erie has never been circumnavigated by any one capable of given an exact account of the bearing

---

[1] Tonawanda Creek.— ED.

[2] The current is six miles an hour at this place.— ED.

of its shores, the depth of its bays, and the anchorages
that occur, or the posts that might be established to
derive advantage from its navigation. The form
which we have given on the map, is according to the
best known memories, from the south part around.[1]

---

[1] We learn from a letter of the Marshal de Belle-Isle, dated July 3,
1758, that M. Pouchot had sent a special map of this lake to M. de
Montcalm who was to send it to that minister. We have found no
copy among M. Pouchot's papers, and it is doubtless lost.— *Note in
Original.*

The following letter to Marshal de Belle-Isle, copied by Mr. Broad-
head from the records of the *Department de la Guerre*, and dated
April 14, 1758, further explains this subject.

"My Lord :— I have handed to the Marquis de Vaudreuil, a map
and memoir, on the subject of the French and English frontiers
which I have drawn up on the best informations I have been able to
procure, during my sojourn at Niagara. I have laid down in my
voyages, the course of the river from Montreal, Lake Ontario as far as
Lake Erie ; therefore it has an appearance of truth which correctly
represents the country and is not contained in any other maps. As
I have not been on the English frontier, I laid that down according
to their best maps, which I again corrected on such reliable information as I have obtained. It is in sufficient detail however, to show
the interest we ought to take to prevent the English interposing obstacles in the way of the Iroquois and Loups, who form a barrier.
That country, my Lord, would be well worth being seen by experi-
enced eyes, which has not yet been the case ; the well known carrying place of Niagara is an evident proof. The most recent accounts
thereof, describe it as the most rugged of Alps, whilst 'tis only a rise
of ground, a little more elevated than that of Bellevue. Below and
above are very fine plains, as can be seen on my map.

The detail of Lake Erie which is entirely unknown ; it is, perhaps,
[as] navigable for large vessels as Lake Ontario. The resources of
those countries once known, would furnish opportunities of avoiding
long routes and expenses, exclusive of enabling us to occupy more
decided points for the security of the country.

If you have the goodness, my Lord, to signify to me that this essay
might please you, I shall set about perfecting that work in order to
accomplish all the objects which will possibly be required of it.

The entrance of the lake, as far as to the Riviere aux Chevaux,[1] forms a great bay lined with flat rock, where no anchorage can be found. If they could keep open the mouth of this river, they would find anchorage for vessels.

The coast from thence to Presque Isle, has no shelter which is known. At Presque Isle, there is a good bay, but only seven or eight feet of water.

Vessels might enter the River à Seguin,[2] and they could make as good a port there as at Sandusky. It is commonly said that the head of the lake is very shallow and the navigation dangerous. What is really the fact is this, that the storms there arise very suddenly, and the waves are so bad, that in rough weather they often kill the fish which are found scattered along the shore. But it is to be observed, that they only navigate this lake in bark canoes, and very seldom in bateaux except from the Niagara River to Presque Isle

---

I hope by my zeal, to deserve the kindness you have promised to honor me with, my Lord, on the recommendation of Mde de Meillian. Since our arrival in this country I have had the good fortune to be always pretty usefully employed. I constructed the Frontenac intrenchments, completed Fort Niagara and the siege of Chouaguen. I dare hope, my Lord, that you will be graciously pleased to give attention to the good reports of me which our generals are so good as to render.

I am, with most profound Respect,

My Lord, Your Most Humble and Most Obed't Serv't,

POUCHOT.

Capt. in the Béarn Regiment."— ED.

[1] Buffalo Creek, which now forms Buffalo Harbor.—ED.

[2] Cuyahoga River, at the mouth of which is the modern city of Cleveland. — ED.

They never go except along the shores which are
shallow, although a little distance out it is deep
enough. It would have been useful to have built a
small vessel with which from the month of May to the
end of September, when the weather is always good, to
sound and reconnoitre all the shelters around the lake,
and then we might build vessels proper for this navigation, which would have saved great labor and expense.

The River Chatacoin is the first that communicates
from Lake Erie to the Ohio, and it was by this, that
they went in early times when they made a journey
in that port. This navigation is always made in a
canoe, on account of the small amount of water in
this river. It is only, in fact, when there is a freshet,
that they can pass, and then with difficulty, which
makes them prefer the navigation of the Riviére aux
Bœufs, of which the entrepôt is the fort of Presque Isle.

This fort is sufficiently large, built piece upon piece,
with buildings for the storage of goods *in transitu*.
It is situated upon a plateau that forms a peninsula
which has given it the name. The country around is
good and pleasant. They there keep wagons for the
portage, which is six leagues. Although in a level
country, the road is not very good to the fort of the
River aux Bœufs, which is square, smaller than the
one at Presque Isle, and also built piece upon piece.[1]

---

[1] The French fort at Au Bœuf was on the site of the village of
Waterford, Erie Co., Pa., thirteen miles from Erie. A small lake and
a stream flowing from it still preserve the name. — ED.

The River aux Bœufs is very crooked and shallow in low water. In rainy weather it swells greatly, and has a rapid current. It is bounded by a valley which becomes deeper as we approach the Ohio.

At its mouth, called in English *Venango*, the French had a very poor, mean fort called *Fort Machault*,[1] which is also an entrepôt for that which is going down to Fort Du Quesne.

The two rivers marked on the map beyond Presque Isle, which fall into the lake, communicate also with rivers that fall into the Ohio, such as the Beaver River. But they are shallow, and besides are embarrassed with rapids.

The River à Séguin has a much better communication with the Ohio. Vessels can go up to within three leagues of its source, and with bateaux they come to a portage not over a mile long.

They then enter a very good river which the English call *Muskingum*. According to accounts it is the finest country in America to live in. They there find the finest timber, suitable for all uses, and the finest lands in the most beautiful plains.

Sandoské also communicates by the River Sonhioto, and the River a la Roche, which descends into the Ohio, with very short portages. This is the great Indian route to come to the Ohio.

---

[1] This fort was on the Alleghany River at the mouth of French Creek, now the village of Franklin, Pa. Venango is a corruption of the word In-nun-gah, by which the Senecas knew the stream. — ED.

21

If we had established ourselves at the two last places above described, instead of going to locate ourselves on the Ohio, we should have intercepted all the communications of the Indians with the English, and would have avoided giving them offence, for until then, they had not been in force to establish themselves where they might wish. The commerce of the Ohio was less than nothing to the French,[1] because this country is only inhabited by the Loups and some Iroquois who are renegades from their own country and have gone to settle there.

The Ohio is navigable almost from its source with canoes, without any rapid. From Kanoagon, the water is always good for bateaux of moderate size. Its course is crooked, and shut in by a valley which deepens and widens as we descend. It has no rapids, but a strong current, especially at high water in the spring.

The navigation, however, requires attention in going down, because the eddies in the river are frequent, and often bear upon trunks of trees, of which its channel is never clear. From Fort Du Quesne, in going down, the navigation becomes better, its bed wider, and the depth of water good.

The valley is not more than a quarter of a league wide, until we reach Fort Du Quesne. The north

---

[1] But the possession of the banks of this river was of the greatest importance to preserve the communication between Canada and Louisiana. — *Note in Original.*

bank is bordered by an elevated but not mountainous country, while the south is the rear of the Apalaches or the Alligeny mountains. There are no navigable rivers coming out of these mountains that communicate with the Ohio, the greater part being rather torrents or brooks than rivers.

The Manenguelée carries bateaux as far up as its fork with the Oxiogani, at the foot of Laurel Hill, or Mount Laurel. Thus far the English have never sought to make these routes except by land.

The mountains on the side of the sources of the Ohio, are rocks covered with bushes like the Cevennes. I have marked upon the map, the routes taken by traders. They take over them horses laden like our pedlars.

Braddock made his road before him from day to day, on his march to the Ohio. But the English re-made it in 1758, and finished it in 1759, as it is marked upon the map.[1]

Fort Du Quesne was upon a low point of land near the river and liable to inundation. The English have built their new fort called Pittsbourg, upon the terrace in front of the old fort. It is a pentagon of about eighty toises on the outside, built of earth, revetted within and without by large pieces of wood, in the same style as that at Oswego. It may contain seven or eight hundred men.

---

[1] See also the march of Colonel Bouquet across the Indian country in 1767, by Thomas Hutchins. — *Note in Original.*

They have built at Loyal-Anon,[1] a fort of upright
timbers, to hold two hundred men. They have also
made in this place a camp entrenched in earth, ten
feet thick at the top, revetted with sticks of wood, and
with a ditch twelve or fifteen feet wide. This camp
was built against a mountain at its foot, and was commanded on every side. The other forts on this route
to Virginia are enclosures of upright timbers, to serve
as storehouses, and will hold garrisons of from twenty-
five to fifty men.

The mountains and the roads of this route are very
difficult. When the English make their convoys, they
are obliged to use a third or more of the horses to
carry the oats for feeding the loaded horses.

The cities for entrepôts for these expeditions, were
Lancaster[2] and Schippenbourg, where they collected all
the provisions and munitions that were to go to the Ohio.

It cannot be doubted but that if the French had
been somewhat in force in these parts, they might
have prevented the enemy from establishing themselves by the strategy of which this mountainous
country is susceptible.

Addition to the Topographical Notices and Observations.

Since M. de la Verandiere, the countries of which
he had knowledge have been visited by Mr. Carver.

---

[1] Legonier. — Ed.

[2] The English count it 338 miles from Pittsbourg to Lancaster, and
66 from Lancaster to Philadelphia. — *Note in Original.*

After having wintered upon the banks of the Mississippi at latitude 44°, he directed his course towards the north of the American continent, and passed by the most elevated regions from whence divide the different rivers which water that country; some flowing to the north sea, others towards the west of the strait of Anian. This English traveler sojourned in the country of the Sakis, the Nadouessis, &c., and was upon the banks of the Bourbon River of Lake Quinipigon, &c. Their existence is therefore no longer a problem. There has been expressed a desire that some one would translate into French the account which Carver published in 1778, of his travels during the years 1766, 1767, 1768. They would give us new light and extend our geographical knowledge. — *Notice added by the Original Editor of Pouchot's Memoirs.*

OBSERVATIONS UPON THE MOUNTAINS OF NORTH AMERICA.

We cannot form a more just idea of the theory of the earth, than by a profound knowledge of the structure and course of mountains. The highest ranges of mountains on our continent for the most part run east and west, while those of North America, as the Cordilleras and Apalachian, on the contrary, have a northerly and southerly course. The academician savans sent to Peru to measure the earth, have furnished M. de Buffon some interesting details upon the Cordilleras, which he has used to establish his theory. He would not have derived the same aid from a report of the Apalaches, which are so to speak forgotten by him. For this reason we here transcribe such judicious observations as we have found, concerning this latter mountain range, from the papers of M. Pouchot, who has profited much from the labors of M. Evans, without, however, citing him.[1]

---

[1] He has sometimes only translated the Analysis of the general map of the British colonies, an English work published in 1755, in 4to, by M. Evans. — *Note in Original.*

The Notre Dame Mountains form a kind of angle at the mouth of the River St. Lawrence, and might be taken for the continuation, or rather the beginning of the Apalachian chain. These mountains are highest towards the mouth of the river, and as we advance into the continent they appear to sink down, and the continent itself rises, till we come to the lakes, where we find plains of very great elevation. These mountains join the eastern end of the Apalaches, of which they form a part.

In the country occupied by the English colonies, the structure of these mountains varies, and they are separated by the Hudson River into two chains, which have a general direction parallel with the sea coast. From the eastern part, till we come to Massachusetts Bay, their course is nearly north and south, but still bearing eastward, following the form of the coast. This tract of country may be divided into two sections, by a line running west from Boston.

The first begins near Watertown, and forms the hills or little mountains, and continues until we have passed Vester,[1] and from thence to within about twenty miles of the Hudson River. The second section is the greater part, and is covered with little mountains which form a long chain, extending towards the south to the sound which separates Long Island from the Main, and forming the slopes, bluffs and detached rocks which

---

[1] Worcester. — ED.

we observe when we sail along the coast of Connecticut, and which prevent them from making good roads into the interior of this country.

Although the greater part of Connecticut might be comprised in this section, we still, however, find large valleys of fine and beautiful country. Among these chains, the greatest are those along the Connecticut River, which are twenty miles apart. The course of the ranges of hills and mountains gives direction to the rivers and streams of this country.

On the east of the first section along the sea shore, the lands are formed by masses of ocean sand mingled with the debris cast up by the tides from the north-east and south-west, which forms almost the whole of Cape Cod, to the east of Massachusetts Bay. Long Island also appears to have been formed by sand from the sea, mingled with the soil brought down by streams from the continent.

The land as we advance westward is of the same description, but the mountains are higher in proportion as we approach the frontiers of Canada.

The country to the south-west of the Hudson, is divided more regularly by a greater number of belts, than the parts of which we have spoken.

The first object we meet in this part, is a bank of rocks of a soft kind of talc, three and even six miles wide, with the summit raised above the adjacent country. It extends south-west from the city of New York, by the lower falls of the Delaware, Schuylkill,

Susquehannah, Gun-Powder, Patapsco, Potomac, Rapahannock, James River and the Roanoack. This chain of rocks, which presents itself as a regular curve, anciently formed the sea shore in this part of America.

From the sea to this chain, and from the Navesink hills to the south-west, as far as the extremities of Georgia, the whole country forms the first belt, and we may designate it as the Low country, being formed of the soil washed down from the upper regions, and mingled with sea sand. These plains are generally not fertilized by any river. The soil is a white sand to a depth of about twenty feet, and entirely sterile, where there is no vegetable mold to improve it. But the parts along the rivers are fertilized by the sediment which they bring down, and which get mingled with the sand, as also the mud from the sea, as the shells and other foreign bodies there demonstrate.

The soil is of this quality over a space forty or fifty miles wide. Along the route from Navesink to Cape Florida, we everywhere discover a sterile country. None of the rivers present a fertile soil adjacent, except where improved by the deposits brought down from above. We only observe marshes or low grounds, scarcely able to support white cedar. We very often meet with veins of clay detached by the sea, from these hills of talc, some of which are three or four miles wide.

From this chain of rocks where all the rivers form

22

a fall, to the broken chain called the South Mountains, there is a tract, fifty, sixty or seventy miles in extent, very uneven, and rising as we penetrate into the interior of the country. This second belt might be termed the Upper country. It consists of strips of different kinds of soil and broken land several miles wide in extent, and thrown up in some places into little ridges and chains of mountains. The slope gives a rapid current to the waters of the torrents and ravines, which wash the soil into the rivers, that fertilize the plains below. These rough slopes, and the ravines render half this country poorly adapted for tillage.

The South Mountains have not any peaks like the Endless Mountains, but they are low, rocky swells, irregularly interrupted, and in some places isolated. Some have a course a few miles long, and others have a breadth of many miles. Between the South Mountains and the high Endless Mountains, which by way of distinction, they call the North Mountains, and in some places the Kittatini and Pequilin, there are some very fine and beautiful valleys of eight, ten and twenty miles wide. It is here that we find the largest part of the best cultivated possessions of the English. This belt crosses New Jersey, Pennsylvania, Maryland and Virginia. No general name has been given to this country, but we might call it *Piedmont*, from its resemblance to that country in Europe, in the goodness of its soil. This is the third belt of North America.

The mountains *Sans-Fin*, or Endless Mountains, so called from the Indian name translated into English, form a long and very uniform chain, about five or six hundred toises high above the intervening valleys. Their name sufficiently describes their extent.

In some places, as towards the Kaatskill, and the sources of the Roanoke, we might imagine that we saw the end of Mount Endless, but if we examine a little in these parts we shall see that they continue in new branches which are not less extensive. Their back chain, which is the Allegany or Ohio River chain, is parallel with the range of talcose rocks which bound the first belt. This chain is terminated by vast peaks of soil and detached rocks towards the sources of the Roanoack, and the New River.

The most easterly chains, which appear to run south, turn imperceptibly to the west making the valleys of the upper belt and of Piedmont, as we have called it, wider in Virginia than in parts further north. The chains to the south-west, appear to blend with the Alleghenies. In some places they are divided, forming new chains of mountains like those of Onasi-oto.

All these mountain chains are penetrated, so to speak by counter-chains or spurs, which come out from the great chains and scatter away as detached peaks, which appear to indicate good passes into the interior but which have no outlets when we try them. It is more sure to pass over the rocks, than the parts where the soil and rocks are blended, because the latter lead into ravines which form precipices. Scarcely a tenth part of the soil in these mountains can be cultivated. This is the fourth belt which borders the Iroquois country and the region which comes down to the plains of the Ohio.

We conclude from these remarks of M. Pouchot; 1st, that all these belts of which he speaks, are only branches of the Apalaches, or rather different portions that compose this chain of mountains, as well in length as in breadth. 2d, that all the country situated east of the Apalaches, has been evidently covered by the waters of the sea, and that the numerous and uneffaceable vestiges of this change prove that this could not have been very ancient.

We may here be allowed to add that this chain of the Apalachian Mountains, and this elevated belt of land on the west, which appears still to retain its ancient limits, is a portion of the principal belt, which stretches from the south-east to north-west, from the mouth of the Rio de la Plata, to and beyond the great lakes of North America.

REMARKS UPON THE FALLS OF NIAGARA.

The most northerly parts of America being very elevated, the rivers which flow from thence must necessarily before discharging themselves into the lakes or rivers, and according to the slope of land, have falls of greater or less size. The most celebrated of all, is without doubt that of Niagara. The Indians near Quebec regarded this as at the western extremity of the continent. When the French came to establish themselves there, they assured them, "that at the end of Lake Ontario, there is a fall which may be a league wide, where an immense body of water falls into the lake, and that beyond this fall there could be seen no more land, neither on one side or the other, but only a sea, so immense that they could see no end, nor say positively that any one had seen it,— that the sun went down on the right hand of this lake, &c."[1]

The journeys which the French undertook at an early period into the interior of America, gave them a

[1] Marc l' Escarbot, Hist. de la Nouvelle France, p. 352.—*Note in Original.*

knowledge less vague concerning this celebrated cascade. They were at first, however, very incorrect, and we can scarcely depend upon the details which the Baron de la Hontan and Father Hennepin had given us. The description which we derive from Father Charlevoix, merits more dependence. M. de Buffon has not hesitated to insert it in his immortal work. Besides what M. Pouchot has related of this fall in the observations which follow, we have found nothing among his papers which we could use.

The river of the Portage, or of the Niagara, is properly nothing but the outlet of Lake Erie, which discharges itself into Lake Ontario, at six leagues from the Falls. It is not easy to measure with instruments the elevation of this fall, and travelers who could see it only in profile, have therefore varied considerably in their accounts. The Baron de la Hontan asserts that they are seven or eight hundred feet high,[1] and the Chevalier de Tonti, a hundred toises.[2] The estimate of Father Charlevoix is much more correct. He gives a hundred and forty or a hundred and fifty feet as the height of the Falls of Niagara.

M. de Buffon had at first supposed this fall was the finest in the whole world, and that it owed this honor to its elevation, but after a little he appears to retract in giving preference to that of Terni in Italy. Al-

---

[1] Voyage, p. 107.— *Note in Original.*

[2] Dern. dec. de l' Amér., p. 30. Father Hennepin gave to this fall a hundred fathoms, that is, six hundred feet.— *Ib.*

though most travelers do not give these falls more than two hundred feet, the illustrious naturalist supposes them to be three hundred.[1] Without seeking to question his evidence, we will only here remark, that the mountain *del Marmore*, has a notch only twenty feet wide, by which the Velino is precipitated, whose vertical fall forms the cascade above mentioned.

It is not the height, but the breadth of a cascade which renders it considerable, and that of Niagara, having nine hundred feet in breadth, evidently surpasses all others. It cannot be compared perhaps with the Terni, which, in relative height, is inferior to several which we know in the country of the Grisons, Valois and Switzerland. We are surprised that M. de Buffon has not cited as perpendicular falls those which occur in the celebrated valley of the Lanterbran, where nature has presented the wildest beauties. From the top of two mountains which terminate with a glacier, and leaving between them a narrow and gloomy valley, there are precipitated some streams which form cascades perhaps the highest in the world. That of Staubbach has been accurately measured, and its vertical height is not less than eight hundred and six royal feet, or eleven hundred feet of Berne. It is true the size is not large, as we may judge by the brook which forms it in falling, and which is scarcely more than

---

[1] Suppl. à l' hist. natur. t. i, p. 469.— *Note in Original.*

eight or nine feet wide. We will not speak of the cascade of Myrrebach, and some others, whose volume of water is also small, and whose elevation is a little less.

The fall of Niagara is also remarkable from the phenomena occasioned by its breadth. When the weather is clear, we always see several rainbows, one within another, of which it is easy to observe the cause. Sometimes a light fog rises like smoke above this cascade, and seems to be a forest on fire. It may be seen from Lake Ontario, fifteen leagues beyond Fort Niagara. This is a certain sign of rain or snow, and a sure means for finding the fort which is at the mouth of the river of the portage.

The noise of the fall, increased by echoes from the surrounding rocks, may be heard a greater or less distance according to the direction of the wind. It is not unusual to hear it ten or twelve leagues, but as a distant thunder, which rolls very heavily. This made Father Charlevoix conjecture, that in time it had formed a cavern under the fall. He gives further as a reason, that nothing ever rises that has once been carried over.[1] The cause of this fact is, that the whirlpools which are always found at the foot of great waterfalls, are in places where the currents of the river are contracted with great force, and are too much drawn together.

---

[1] *Journal Hist. du Voyage de l'Amérique Sept. t.* v; *de l'hist. de la Nouvelle-France*, p. 346. — *Note in Original.*

An anxiety to criticise the Baron de la Hontan, has led Father Charlevoix to deny that fish which are often drawn into the rapids above, are killed in the fall. "They have further assured me," says this Jesuit, "that birds flying over, are sometimes enveloped in the whirlwinds formed in the air by the violence of the rapid. But I have observed to the contrary, as I have seen little birds flying very low, directly above the fall and come out uninjured.[1] "We have ourselves seen birds plunge in below the cascade of the Rhine, by the side of the chateau of Lauffen, forty feet high, and then fly away safely.[2] Birds of prey might be shot very easily at Niagara in calm weather, but not when the winds are strong in the south bend. Then, as M. Pouchot has observed many times, aquatic birds which follow the course of the river and hover over the rocks, are compelled to find shelter by flying near the surface of the water, but not being able in this position to resist the currents of air, they are precipitated into the basin. It is much the same with the fish that are drawn into the rapids above the falls, which are sensible as far as Lake Erie. A great many animals also perish in the vortices of the water, which are so dreadful above the falls that they cannot swim them.[3] Ten or twelve Outaouais Indians, having wished to cross at

---

[1] *Id.* p. 346, 347. — *Note in Original.*

[2] On the opposite side near the forges of Neuhaussen this fall appears lower. — *Ib.*

[3] *Trans. Philos. t.* vi, Part II, p. 119. — *Ib.*

this part of the river in their canoes to escape from a
party of the Iroquois who were pursuing them, made
vain efforts to resist the impetuosity of the currents,
which did not hinder them from being engulphed in
the falls.[1]

Although the mass of waters falls vertically upon
the rocks, there has formed, notwithstanding, by the
strong impulse of the current and its great volume, a
considerable talus. Baron de la Hontan pretends that
below there is a path where three men might easily
pass from one side to the other without being wet, or
even getting a drop of water upon them.[2] Neither
Father Charlevoix nor M. Pouchot speak of this path,
and probably no one would like to try it.

Around the falls we observe the banks eighty
feet high, which indicate plainly that the channel
which the river has formed, was formerly almost on a
level with Lake Erie. The falls of Niagara ought to
have then been much higher than at present, and the
bed of rock which exists, has been worn little by little
to bring it to its present form.

When we come to the top of the neighboring mountains near the falls, we find a plain three or four leagues
wide, which extends from the shores of Toronto
around Lake Ontario, varying according to the trend
of the shore, to the north-east and south-west. This

------

[1] *Charlevoix Jour.*, cit. p. 345. — *Note in Original.*
[2] *Voy.* p. 107. — *Ib.*

terrace or chain of hills begins at the northern mountains, and extends eastward into the country of the
Five Nations. We cannot doubt but that these hills
once formed the lake shore, and that its waters have
gradually subsided, leaving the plains that surround it.

The extent of all the great lakes, and especially that
of Lake Erie, which is above the falls of Niagara, has
undergone the same change. The banks of the River
St. Lawrence, which is their outlet, has not been
exempt from this change. The Island of Montreal,
formed by two branches of this river, furnishes us the
proof of this. Its ridges are elevated considerably
above its shores, and show by this, that all the grounds
from their foot to the river bank were formerly covered
by its waters which have gradually receded in proportion as the volume of the lakes has diminished by the
gradual lowering of Niagara Falls and the other rapids
or cascades that interrupt the course of the river above
Montreal.

We also report a proof of change of which we will
speak. If we seek upon the highest mountains in
Canada, we shall everywhere find sea shells of every
sort, as well as in the ancient plains covered with limestone, sulphurous rock, shales and sandstones. The
more recent plains are on the contrary filled with petrifactions of wood, fruits, serpents, snails, and various
fresh water shells.

ON THE CUSTOMS AND MANNERS OF THE INDIANS OF NORTH AMERICA.

NOTICE.

We owe to the Missionaries many precious details concerning the customs and manners of the Indian tribes of North America, although we doubtless should have less occasion to reproach these apostles of the New World, had they allowed themselves to be less subjugated by the prejudices of the State, by whom they have been too often influenced according to its peculiar interests, either to exaggerate the barbarism of the Indians, or to disguise their faults. One of them, Father Lafitau, has not hesitated to compare them with the first nations of antiquity. His imagination has led him to trace many resemblances in religion, customs, traditions, &c. Few persons can now recognize the reality of such parallels, notwithstanding the fashion for such reasoning in the present age.

The first travelers, and especially Champlain, the founder and father of the French Colony of Canada, have given their accounts with that simplicity and truth, that will render them always valuable, although the style may be almost unintelligible. Those who followed them, instead of rectifying their errors, have multiplied them, or have disguised their accounts. Some have even dared to extol the Indians, in a manner as ridiculous as it is absurd. Had they only pretended to write a satire upon civilized nations, they might possibly have been pardoned; but they have attempted to deceive their cotemporaries, and to cheat posterity.

The Baron de la Hontan, especially deserves censure. He has wished to transform all the natives of America into great philosophers, and, unfortunately, his work has hitherto enjoyed a dangerous celebrity. Jean Jacques Rousseau has from thence derived many of his ideas, as false as they are foreign.

A minister of Cleves, with whom paradoxes cost nothing, and who always decides wrong and contrary, when he stops reasoning badly, has, without going out of Germany, thought it necessary to reject indiscriminately all the testimony of missionaries and travelers, to give credit to his own reveries. As these have misled many readers, and might possibly appear to throw unjust prejudices upon the statements of M. Pouchot, we deem it necessary to here transcribe the opinion of M. de Buffon, concerning the system of this minister M. Pauw.[1] It is an excellent

---

[1] Recherches Philosophiques, sur les Américaines, ou Memoires interessans pour servir a l'Histoire de l'Espece Humaine. Par, M. de *Pauw*, Berlin, 2 vols. 8vo., 1768; 3 vols. 12mo. 1770.— Ed.

antidote to the work of this bold detractor of the human race.

"I confess," says this illustrious naturalist, "that I have not sufficient knowledge,[1] to be able to confirm these facts, which I would have doubted less, had not this author advanced a great number of others which are absurd, or directly opposed to the best known and proven facts. I scarcely need to cite here his statements that the Mexican and Peruvian monuments have no existence,—yet their ruins are yet standing, and prove by their grandeur the genius of these people, whom he treats of as stupid beings, degenerated from the human race, as much in form as in understanding. It appears that M. Pauw has sought to bring every thing to support his views, and that he has chosen his facts to this end. I am ashamed that a man of merit, who otherwise appears to be well informed, should have yielded to this excessive partiality in his judgment, and that he should have chosen to rely upon equivocal facts.

Is it not the height of absurdity to blame severely those travelers and naturalists who have ventured to advance some questionable statements, while he himself presents those still more incredible? He admits and advances such statements as might favor his

---

[1] How different is this language from that of M. Pauw! Should not a foreign author who writes in our language, afford to assume an honest and moderate tone, when the first writer of the nation is always making his apologies? — *Note in Original.*

opinions, and he asks us to believe them upon his word, without citing his proofs; as for example, upon frogs, which he says bellow like a calf,—upon the flesh of the iguana, which gives the syphilis to those who eat it,—upon the glacial coldness of the earth at one or two feet in depth, &c.[1] He pretends that the Americans in general are degenerated men, as it is not possible to conceive that there could have been beings at the first creation, in a state of decrepitude and decay, such as the Americans are;—that there are no shells, nor other debris of the sea upon the high mountains, nor even upon those of moderate height;—that there were no cattle[2] in America before its discovery;—that no one who has properly reflected upon the constitution of the climate of America can help regarding the people of this continent as very recent;—that beyond the eightieth degree of latitude, beings organized like ourselves could not breathe during the twelve months of the year, on account of the density of the atmosphere;—that the Patagonians are of a stature equal to that of Europeans, &c.

---

[1] In the town of Brandon, Vt., a stratum of frozen gravel has been found fourteen feet below the surface.—*Geological Survey of Vermont*, i, 192. Other localities of ice caves, frozen wells, &c., have been described. Although extremely rare, it is possible that the early travelers may have noticed some one of these localities, and from thence have inferred that they were of common occurrence.—ED.

[2] The term *bœuf*, here used, may possibly have been intended for buffalo.—ED.

But it is useless to make a further enumeration of all these false statements, or conjectures which this author affirms with a confidence which offends every reader who loves the truth. *Supplem. à l'hist. nat. Tom.* viii, ed. in 12, p. 326, 327, 328, 329.

On the Manners and Customs of the Indians.

The race of men who people this great continent is the same everywhere, with but slight differences. They are generally copper colored, and commonly appear to be darker because they are brought up naked, and from their custom of rubbing their skin with grease, potter's clay or brown colors, which, joined with their filthiness, renders them still blacker than they would naturally be. They have a very distinctive mark, in not having either beard or eyebrows. It is true they take care to pull out such as come, but these are only scattered hairs. If they are now found with a little beard, it is only because they are mixed with European blood.

They are commonly large. Their stature is five feet four, five or six inches, and upwards to six feet. They are very active. Some have a prepossessing appearance, and in several nations we observe the airs of a dandy. They have a quick eye, and generally they have less strength than Europeans. The women have forms less well proportioned, and they become very fat, and fade at an early age. There are some nations on the side of the Chaouanous, which are whiter, and some even as much so as the Germans, but this is very rare.

Those who differ in figure, chiefly do so by artificial means. The Flat Heads and all the Caraibes, have a forehead flat, and the upper part of the head elevated, because in infancy their heads are tied between two pieces of wood. Those called Têtes de Boule have a round head, which is peculiar to several nations in the north-west part of America. It is said that they find in that part, men with beards, but this is very doubtful. No one has seen them except the Indians, who might have taken the Spaniards for the natives of the country, as they occupy in those parts. It is a striking fact, that those accustomed to see Indians, can judge of their traits, so that by their manner of acting, they can tell to what nation they belong, without speaking with them.

Each nation may be regarded as a family assembled in the same canton. The different nations very rarely go among one another, and each one inhabits a separate canton of this great continent. Unless their national interest requires it, or the wars they undertake make it necessary, they travel but little, and remain separately in their own districts. Each nation is divided into villages, which do not resemble those of Europe. An Indian village has its cabins scattered along a river or a lake, and sometimes extends one or two leagues. Each cabin holds the head of the family, the children, grand-children, and often the brothers

24

and sisters, so that there are sometimes as many as
sixty persons. This cabin usually forms a very elongated square, of which the sides are not more than
five or six feet high. It is made of elm bark, and the
roof is the same, with an opening along the top to let
out the smoke, and an entrance at both ends without
a door. We may infer from this, that they are always
full of smoke. They build the fire under the hole in
the roof, and they have as many fires as they have
families. The pot is held up by two crotches, and a
stick of wood laid across, with a pot ladle called a
mikoine at the side.

The beds are upon some planks on the ground, or
upon simple hides which they call *appichimon*, placed
along the partitions. They sleep upon these skins,
wrapped in their blankets, which by day serves them
for clothing. Each one has his particular place. The
man and wife sleep crouched together, her back being
against his body, their blankets passed around their
heads and feet, so that they look like a plate of ducks.
The cabins of the Scioux, on the great plains of the
Mississippi, are formed like a cone, by poles covered
with skins of the buffalo wrapped around them, which
gives them a very pleasing effect.

Although the Indians who have been domiciliated
or christianized, have lost none of their customs, yet
they are, however, lodged more conveniently than the
others, at the king's expense. They there even have
some rooms furnished to receive Europeans when they

come to see them. Their furniture consists of pots of various sizes according to their need. Their clothing is a shirt, that is cut for men. Their women wear the same. They are fond of finery. Young people are dandies, and the women are fond of wearing ruffles bordered with lace. They never take them off until they are used up or spoiled. At first these are white, then from rubbing with vermillion they are red for some time, and finally they become black from use. We may judge from this, that the consumption is very great, as they never wash them. They ordinarily take off their garments upon going to bed. The men sleep entirely naked; the women wear only the *machicote*, for sake of decency. Their stockings are a kind of gaiter, made of flannel cloth fringed with red, white or blue. This gaiter is sewed up following the shape of the leg, with four fingers' breadth of stuff outside of the seam. This strip is bordered with ribbons of different colors, mingled with designs in glass beads, which forms a very pleasing effect, especially when the leg is not too short and thick, which is rarely seen among them. Besides this, they wear garters of beads, or porcupine quills, bordered four fingers' wide, which are tied on the side of the leg. The bands of the gaiters hang almost in front to cover the legs against the brush. Their shoes are a kind of slipper made of stag or deer-skin, tanned like goat skin and very soft. On the top of the foot it is laced and covered with fringe, and at the ancle it is two fingers'

wide, and also bordered with porcupine quills dyed of
different colors, and furnished with little pendants of
copper having tufts of colored hair, and with little bells,
which tinkle as they walk. This use may perhaps
have been suggested for the purpose of avoiding the
serpents and adders, which occur in great numbers.
They also have shoes for winter use formed like laced
boots, which are very good, and cost almost a Louis a
pair, the cheapest being from forty sous to three livres.
We sometimes see pairs of gaiters which cost as much
as thirty livres. The women wear an under petticoat
called *machicote*, made of an ell of blue or red cloth of
the quality like that of Berri or of Carcassonne. The
lower edge is ornamented with several strips of yellow,
blue and red ribbon or English edging lace. This
arrangement resembles a courrier's frock. It is fastened around the waist by a strap. The shirt passes
over and covers this. These women are loaded with
collars like decorated virgins. They are ribbons of
wampum or bead work, to the ends of which are
attached Calatrava crosses, and some have sewed upon
them pieces of money, that hang down below the
neck and almost cover it.

They do not pierce their ears like the men, but they
wear chains made of brass or beads, which descend
very low upon the shoulders. They wear their hair
parted in the middle of the forehead, and so arranged
as to cover a part of their ears, and fastened behind
by a queue, which falls down to the waist. This queue

which is is haped like a lobster's tail, is about four
inches wide above and three below, and somewhat flat.
It is covered with an eel skin, wrapped around it, and
colored red. Some have this ornamented above with
a plate of silver two or three fingers' breadth wide, and
below by little triangles, also of silver, or something
else, which does not give a bad effect. A woman
who should have this queue cut off, would feel herself
dishonored, and would not venture to show herself
until it might have time to grow again. The hair of
the women serves them to wipe their hands continually
of everything greasy that they touch. It is very black,
long, sleek and thick. They sometimes put vermillion
into the streak where the hair is parted, and behind
their ears. The Abenakies paint the whole face, when
they are fully arrayed, reddish brown above, and vermillion below.

The Outaouaises often wear instead of shirts, a kind
of waistcoat of blue or red cloth, cut in two pieces, so
that with four or six cords they can cover a half of the
body and the arms.

The men instead of a machicote, wear a breech-
cloth, which is a quarter of an ell of cloth, which they
pass under the thighs, crossing before and behind upon
a belt around the waist. Sometimes this cloth is em-
broidered. When they travel, to avoid being chafed
by the cloth, they put it on simply as an apron before
them. They wear around the neck, a collar pendant
like our orders of knighthood. At the end is a plate of

silver, as large as a saucer, or a shell of the same size, or a disc of wampum.[1]

The fore arm is ornamented with silver broaches, three or four fingers wide, and the arms by a kind of wristlets made of wampum or colored porcupine quills with fringes of leather above and below.

The Indians are fond of wearing rings upon all their fingers. The men's heads are more ornamented than those of the women, and they will sometimes spend three or four hours at their toilet. They may be said to be more attached to this than any dandy in France. The practice of dressing their faces artistically in red, black and green, in fanciful designs, and which they often change two or three times a day, does not allow us to judge the natural color except of the eyes and teeth, which are small but very white. The lips are stained with vermillion. They do not wear the hair longer than a priest's calotte, cut an inch long, covered with grease and powdered with vermillion in the middle. They leave two locks of hair, which they fasten by two silver clasps of a finger's length, or in a queue made with a border of porcupine quills. They arrange therein also, some feathers of birds, forming a kind of tuft. When a young man

---

[1] The wampum [*Porcelaine*] of Canada, is made of shells which the English call clams, which are found on the shores of New England and Virginia. They are tapering, elongated, somewhat pointed and quite thick. See the Journal of Father Charlevoix, vol. v, of the *History of New France*, p. 308; *Voyage of Kalm in North America*, vol. ii, p. 385, *et seq. — Note in Original*.

has been to war, he cuts the border of his ears, and attaches a piece of lead so that the weight may elongate the cartilage, forming an opening large enough to put in a *mitasse*[1] rolled up. They put in a brass wire around, and in the circumference they put in tufts of colored hair or feathers. These ears come down upon their shoulders, and float there as they walk. When they travel in the woods, they put a band around the forehead to keep their ears from being torn in the thickets. They do not keep their ears till they become wise, because in quarreling while drunk, they tear them, so that before getting far along in life they lose them entirely. They pierce the cartilage of the nose, and put in a little ring with a triangle of silver, which falls down before the mouth.

Both men and women wear a blanket on their shoulders, either of wool which they buy of Europeans, or of cloth or prepared skins. Those in the interior can scarcely provide anything for themselves besides the latter. Those of wool, are blankets made in Normandy of very fine wool, and better than those supplied by the English, which are coarser. For children they are of the size of one point, or one point and a half. For men, they are two or three points. After having carried them white two or three days, they mark them in vermillion, at first with a red cross. Some days after, they cover them with red, which tends to make

[1] Moccasin. — ED.

the skin red. When the maidens have some design
of conquest, they paint their blankets anew. The
cloth of the latter is an ell and a quarter, of red or blue
stuff of the same quality as the *machicotes*. They
ornament the lower part with a dozen strips of yellow,
red or blue ribbon and English edging, leaving the
breadth of a ribbon between the rows. At the end of
these bands they leave five or six fingers' breadth of
the ribbons hanging free. They are fastened above
with round silver buckles, three-fourths of an inch
across. This is the arrangement of the beaux and
belles. The men prefer to wear capotes or a kind of
laced coat, with a false cap on the border, the sides
held with buttons, and further adorned with blue, yellow or red feathers. They have never been willing to
wear breeches, not even the Christians, notwithstanding the solicitation of the missionaries. Imagine a
shirt almost black, and powdered in red, a waistcoat
laced or with tinsel glazing, a laced coat unbuttoned,
a cap untied, sometimes a wig put on wrong side
before, joined with a face to which a Venetian mask
could not compare in singularity, and you will have
an idea of the costume of an Indian. The men wear
a belt about six inches wide, made of wool of different
colors, which the Indian women make very neatly,
with flaming designs. They hang to this belt their
mirrors and their tobacco pouch, which is the skin of
an otter, beaver, cat or bird, taken off whole and
tanned, into which they put their pipe, tobacco and

steel. They have also a pocket hanging like a little wallet, for carrying their balls and lead for hunting or war. They carry their mirror and tomahawk upon their hips. They have an ox horn with a shoulder strap for carrying powder. Their knife is hung in a sheath from the neck, and falls upon the breast. They also have a crooked knife, which is a blade of a knife or a curved sword, and they make great use of this. Such are the implements and riches of the Indians, and they regard this property as sacred as their children.

The women and girls stay out of their cabins during the menstrual period, and remain until it is over and they have washed. During this time the Indians do not cohabit with them, and but seldom during pregnancy or while nursing. The women are commonly delivered alone. They go out of the cabin and crouch down upon some boughs of trees. They never groan, and think strange that European women should utter cries at such a time.

They at once go with their infants to wash them in the water, and then return to their cabins, notwithstanding which, bad cases seldom occur in their accouchements.

Both men and women show a great attachment for their children. The latter have a particular regard for them, and manage them very properly. Their cradle is a plank, upon which they wrap the infant in the softest skins. They place under a soft cushion

25

prepared from rushes, so as not to chafe from its
ordure, and take care to leave a little opening in front,
so arranged that the child can urinate externally. If
it is a girl, they fix a little channel of bark. The
plank has holes on the sides to pass bands for wrapping up the child. The feet have a little rest. Above
the head is a hoop three fingers' breadth wide, upon
which they fasten a curtain of calico or such other
suitable cloth as they may have to cover the child.

At the top of the plank they attach a strap for carrying the child. They pass it over in front, when the
cradle hangs along their shoulders. If the child cries
they sooth it by rocking, and when it stops they hang
it to some branch, in such a way that the child is
always upright. It sleeps in this position with the
head resting upon its shoulders. When it is sick, the
mother holds it lying down, and never goes out of its
sight, and gives it little remedies which are good for
it. If they give an enema, they use a bladder with a
little pipe inserted in its neck. The Indian women
nurse their children two or three years or more, for
they quit the breast of their own accord. They go
entirely naked till they are four or five years old. At
this age the girls wear only a *machicote*. All the children of both sexes have a little blanket. They shout,
weep and play among themselves without their
parents paying any attention to them. It is seldom
that they quarrel. When it is necessary to carry
them, the child embraces the mother's neck, and

straddles its legs across her shoulders. It is held in a blanket, in which it reposes. Men, women and children of some size are charged with this care. When they travel by land, each one carries a little packet upon his shoulders suspended to the forehead by a collar. This bundle is done up in a blanket folded at the two ends by the strings of the belt and lashed very firmly like a purse.[1]

The children until thirteen or fourteen years of age, have nothing to do but to play. The boys make little bows, using strips of wood with a ball at the end, and amuse themselves in shooting little birds, at which they become so adroit that they often kill them. Their favorite game is cricket, at which both great and small amuse themselves. Sometimes from twenty to fifty persons play at a time, and they sometimes lose in play all their goods. Whatever harm may happen as sometimes occurs, from the eagerness in which they play, they never take offense at it.

The girls at first amuse themselves in making dolls. They are then employed in soaking and preparing skins. This life of idleness gives them an early slyness, and sometimes at six or eight years of age, they have lost their virginity in playing with other children. Their parents have nothing to blame, saying that every one is the master of his or her own person. The girls,

---

[1] This would be a very good practice for our soldiers. The English have adopted it.— *Note in Original.*

however, always preserve an air of decency in the way of speech and deportment. They will allow no one to touch their necks nor to kiss them, especially in the day time, and in public, are always much enveloped in their blankets, and they walk by taking very short steps. They carry their feet straight forward and not outward, and walk like little mistresses. The men walk with their feet very much turned inward, perhaps from the practice of traveling in the woods, which forms this custom to prevent them from not striking the roots. The girls who are of a temperament follow it, while others remain discreet, and also from preference.

The boys when fourteen years old begin to hunt, and even go to war. The amusement of the young people in the villages is dancing, in which they are sometimes engaged until two or three hours after midnight. The girl who has a fancy for a young man, places herself behind him in the dance, and follows him all the evening. These dances are performed in a ring; the step of the men is almost like that of the Germans, and that of the women a very short movement. Their singing is commonly very free, the head one singing while the rest reply by a *héé*, in final cadence. At the end of each strophe they all finish by a general cry, after which they make a short pause, and then take up another couplet, the women not saying a word. They dance with so much vivacity that it throws them all into a perspiration. These dances appear well calculated to fortify the health, while that of the Europeans is not so fatiguing. They have other dances of ceremony, which are executed by the men, and of which we shall elsewhere speak.

These dances being finished, those that find themselves without notice, retire to their cabins to sleep. The others do not go thither, and the girl follows the youth without saying any thing, to the place where he is going to sleep. When he is in bed, he says to her, "lie down." Then the latter disrobes, and gently crawls under his blanket, which she arranges with her own in the manner of wrapping up already noticed. They often lie until nine or ten o'clock in the morning, after which they converse no more during the day. Sometimes he who has a fancy for a maiden, will wait till she has retired to her cabin and every thing is still. He then enters, goes to the fire, and takes a small burning coal, which he carries to her face. If she draws her head under the blanket, he retires without speaking, but if on the contrary she blows the coal, he throws it down, and lies down by her side.[1]

The young men are usually more discreet than the young women, and we often find those twenty-two or twenty-three years old, who have not wished to know them, saying that they did not wish to weaken themselves. It is even indecent for a young man to make love to a girl. They do not esteem a man unless he is

[1] This they call *souffler l'allumette*, [blowing the coal.] — *Note in Original.*

sought, and those who run after women are not re-
spected among them.   Although they have some discreet young women, there are, however, but few who
are able to resist their inclinations or a present, and
they hold in great vanity the price, taking occasion to
boast of their good luck, and of what has been given
them, especially as regards the European chiefs of consideration among them, whom they could scarcely
resist.   They prefer an Indian to a European, and it is
commonly interest or vanity that gives favor to the
latter.   If the latter regards some one with consideration, she will tell it in her family, who will come and
return thanks for the honor he has done them.

If they have a true inclination, they become very
jealous, and the result may be quite tragic.   If they
love their lovers, they take up with care and pride the
fruit of their love, otherwise the mother turns away
from it, and sometimes poisons it.   As soon as a
couple is arranged, the other girls take care not to
look after this man, and send him to his mistress.   If
any one gets away their lovers, they will then fight for
them.

We may assume that there are three ways of making
love among the Indians :   1st, Love in the ring, which
originates in the dance, a present, &c.   2d, That of inclination, or that resulting from a kind of hired marriage.
3d, That of those who engage to contract a legitimate
marriage.   The first and second are of no account with
them, and do not prevent them from thinking of the

latter. Many young women prefer to remain in the
public service. Those who live in this libertine way,
are very subject to miscarriage. Notwithstanding this
licentious life, where they find nothing to care for but
to eat and drink, they nevertheless respect themselves
as between brother and sister. The Iroquois even
regard cousins-germain as brothers, and do not wish to
have any relations with those so near. If asked the
reason, they reply that such is their usage. There are,
however, nations on the side of the Sauteurs or Ochibois, who, when some one has married a daughter in a
family, regards all her sisters as his wives. The Outaouais and Mississakes take as many as two or three, if
they think they can support them by the chase, which
is not common. When asked why they have but one
wife, they reply that it is for the peace of the family,
for if one is preferred, the jealousy of the others occasions disputes, which the husband is obliged to settle
with a club. If a girl has a decided inclination for a
young man, she finds out where he is; if he is traveling, she takes his pack and carries it. If the young
man has a liking for her, he takes her to the chase
with him, and she serves him as a wife all this time.
He takes care of her, and on their return sometimes
quits her, and at other times they remain married.
The women think, as among the Turks, that they were
created for the service of man, and to relieve them of
their domestic cares. The Indians sometimes marry
from inclination, but almost always from family in-

terest, to form an alliance, or to acquire a hunter in the family, the husband going to live in the cabin of the wife. It is therefore advantageous to have girls in a house, since when they marry, it is with hunters, for the relief of their fathers and mothers. Many young people do not marry in order to serve in this way their own parents when they become old.[1]

The marriage ceremony is short. If it is a marriage for the convenience of the parents, the relatives propose the alliance among themselves and then notify their children. If they have a liking one to another, the youth goes to live in the cabin of the maid, and presents her an entire outfit. When he has laid down, he proposes to her to lie down with him. She is standing by his side near the couch, and after being urged for some time, she disrobes and modestly gets into the bed. Among the Iroquois, it is a mark of consideration not to touch the woman, and they sometimes thus remain as much as three months, to indicate in a more marked degree how much they esteem them.[2] The husband brings all the peltries of the chase to his wife, who prepares the skins for their common use, and she ordinarily makes the sale, and receives in exchange whatever is needful for the family, and the surplus in jewels of the kind which we shall describe, together

[1] Among the Iroquois the line of descent is always on the side of the woman. They say that such a one is the son of such a woman, designating the family by the mother's name.— *Note in Original.*

[2] In what country, and among what people, has not nature been outraged by opinion? — *Ib.*

with the brandy which they sell again in their cantons, or drink in their ceremonies. The husband assumes to purchase arms and munitions. The women become very discreet, and always accompany their husbands as well as the family, except when they go to war. The women are charged with the cultivation of Indian corn, and of preparing it, and have charge of the kettle; besides which, they go to get wood, and to bring in the wild beasts which are killed in the vicinity of the cabin. Often the husband will come in, and without speaking a word, light his pipe. After some time, he will tell his wife, that he has killed such a beast, at about such a place in the woods. As he has made some blows with his hatchet upon the trees along the route, the woman goes off and brings in the spoils upon her shoulders.[1]

The woman's life is laborious. If her temper does not agree with that of the husband, they separate and divide their children. The mother takes by preference the girls. If she is much displeased with her husband, she will take charge of all the children, who are their treasures, and very often they marry again immediately.

The long separation of the husband from the wife, especially among young people, occasioned by pregnancy and lactation, sometimes occasions divorces, because they get tired of being alone. This is usually

---

[1] An European could scarcely find a place thus designated.— *Ib.*

26

the time they take for going to war. In this interval
they find others whom they marry, and it is not unusual to find those who have five or six wives, while
others content themselves through their whole lives
with one. Jealousy also occasions divorces. If they
suspect that their women are wanting in conjugal
fidelity, they cut their noses with their teeth, and send
them away, but these examples are very rare.

The Scioux have a punishment still more remarkable. When they wish to punish a woman for adultery,
they assemble as many young men as they can, sometimes thirty or forty, and after a great festival, they
give up the woman to them to enjoy at their discretion,
and then abandon her, and some one kills her. This
ceremony they call, *faire passer par la prairie.* Some
others kill them. We may be assured that infidelity
among women is very rare, and many less people have
occasion to complain of this than in Europe.

When the Indian women become old, which happen
early, and at about forty years of age, they are without
claims. They acquire, however, much consideration,
and are consulted in difficult affairs especially among
the Iroquois, by whom they are called women of counsel. They, in fact, enter into the grand councils of the
nations. They never declare war without consulting
them, and only resolve upon it in accordance with their
advice. Upon these occasions they exhort their warriors to conduct themselves bravely, and to display to
the whole world that they are men able to protect

them. They especially enjoin it upon them not to abandon their wounded.

The Indians are not altogether occupied by the chase when in their villages. They neither hunt nor fish except to live. During the sojourn that they make, they assemble in their cabins, almost always that of their chief, where with calumet in mouth, they discuss their politics, and rehearse the history of their nation. They then speak of treaties, of the interests they have in foreign nations, and the journeys they have made in their wars. The young people, already grown, listen, in order to put themselves in readiness for business, and there acquire that emulation for war, which is the most essential object of their lives. The most aged are the chiefs of the council, and it is these that direct the war. The Indians who are from thirty to forty years old, conduct the young warriors. From want of subsistence, the Indians do not remain always in their villages. They only raise Indian corn enough to last two or three months. As soon as they begin to find themselves in need, the whole family goes to establish itself at a distance, especially if they are intending to remain for a long time. In the winter time these villages are found most frequently abandoned, especially by those nations that are the greatest hunters of the beaver. They scatter themselves all through the interior of the country which they regard as belonging to their nation, and live quite isolated along the lakes, ponds or rivers, where they think they can find the most game. Upon arriving at their destination, they build a cabin, which is always placed in some thicket or valley, so as to be sheltered from the winds. They gather a pile of wood for stormy winter days, and the husband and young persons disperse themselves around the cabin to hunt, sometimes to a distance of ten leagues. They put nets under the ice to catch the beaver, or when found outside, they kill them with a gun. They hunt the bears which they find in hollow trees, and which they distinguish by the bark. If they find any within, they are believed to be ruminating or licking their paws. They throw fire into the hole to make them come out, or build one at the foot which smokes them out. The bear pressed by the fire and the smoke, comes out of the trunk, where he is upright, and as soon as they see him upon the tree they fire, and sometimes they are obliged to cut down the tree to get him. They fix traps or snares for taking foxes, otters and martens. They also kill lynxes, pole-cats, pécans, wild cats, muskrats, wood-rats, caribous, moose,[1] deer, (of which the greatest hunting is done in summer), stags, hedge-hogs, partridges, (which are the wood hens of Europe), and turkeys, which are very plenty in certain places. They eat the meat of all these animals except foxes, otters and pécans. They also place nets under the ice to catch fish. They cut these animals into pieces, after having properly skinned

---

[1] These two latter kinds of animals are quite rare. — *Note in Original.*

them, and put the quarters of the meat upon a kind of frame work which they form over their fires, to dry and cure it in the smoke. This meat serves them for those days when they are not successful in hunting, or when the stormy weather compels them to stay in their cabins. One would believe from an enumeration of the animals which we have made, that the Indians should live a happy life; but their indolence, bad weather and the scarcity of game in some parts, sometimes reduces them to the most extreme necessities, and compels them to seek for roots to live upon, and often even these are wanting. They then have been so reduced as to eat their prisoners, or even one another, the distance of all succors, bad weather and frozen rivers having detained them in spite of their efforts, in the districts where they happened to be found. They often change their dwellings to find a place nearer their hunting.

When the severe cold has passed, and the ice begins to thaw, nature is soon in motion, and the trees which have been frozen, have a water between the inner bark and the wood, which is not the juice of the tree, but precedes it about a month. When an incision is made a little obliquely, and they have fitted in a knife blade, or the end of a bark, a water flows from this wound, which when boiled, produces a kind of chrystaline substance, which is bitter or sweet according to the quality of the trees. That of the walnut[1] and cherry, is of the

---

[1] The sap of the walnut is sweet, like that of the maple.— ED.

former kind.   Almost all the trees yield this water,
which might be made of some use, even for medicine.
The maple and the plane-tree or sycamore have a
water so sweet that it forms a very good sugar.   It is
equally sweet and refreshing, and very healthy for the
lungs.   When they boil it down, it forms a kind of
damp sugar, or little cakes of reddish sugar, which has
somewhat the taste of manna, but very agreable, and
of which we may eat as much as we please without
fear of any bad result, like the sugar from cane.   The
Indians, who at that season can neither hunt nor fish,
on account of the melting of the ice, and as the fish
have not yet begun to run up the rivers, live upon
this manna during fifteen days or a month.

These trees give plentifully of this liquor, which only
runs when it freezes at night and thaws by day.   But
if the sky is covered, or it should rain, the trees would
not flow.   This is a curious observation for the naturalists.   They collect this juice in a kettle or a little
wooden trough, once or twice a day, and they can
keep it for some time.   They then boil it in large
cauldrons, and the granular substance which it forms
is the sugar.   It is excellent for colds.   They make a
very good syrup with the capillaire,[1] although it has a
taste like that of burnt paper.   It is also good for all
kinds of sweet meats, makes chocolate excellent, and

---

[1] A fern known to botanists as the *Adiantum pedatum*, or Maiden's-
hair, common throughout the Northern States and Canada.— ED.

agrees very well with milk and coffee, to which, however, it imparts a disagreable medicinal taste. There is no doubt but that we could find this same sugar in Europe, especially after cold winters, if we should seek for it when the buds are a little swelled on the trees.

When the ice melts, the Indians find many swans, geese, bustards, ducks, teals, plovers, woodcock, and snipe, which return to the southern part of America to repeople that country. We cannot describe the prodigious quantities which are found at this season, until they get settled in the great ponds and marshes where they build their nests.

At the same time the fish begin to come out of the great lakes to go up the rivers, and as nearly all of these have a kind of little canal at their mouths, where it is usually not more than two, three, or four feet deep, the Indians watch at these passages to spear them, at which they become very adroit. The quantities that go up on some days is inconceivable. The carp appears first, of which there are two kinds, one like that of Europe but better, and another kind which has knobs upon the head. They call them *galeuses*. They are fat and very good, being from six to ten pounds in weight. Then comes the barbue,[1] which is a flat headed fish, with four large barbs on the side of the mouth. It has the flavor and color of the tench, and weighs from two to seven pounds. The sturgeons

---

[1] The *Pimelodus*, or cat fish, of which there are several species common in the waters of Canada.— ED.

are from five to seven feet long.   About the months of
May and June they find pike, weighing from seven to
fifteen pounds, mullet, and salmon trout of from fifteen
to eighteen pounds, and achigans gilded and green.
This latter fish is short, flat and more delicate than all
the others.   The mastilongé, which grows to from ten
to twenty-five pounds, is a kind of pike-trout, and very
good, as also the gilded fish, which is shaped like a
cleaving axe, is good flavored and weighs from five to
twelve pounds.   They find all kinds of European fish,
such as perch, of three and four pounds, eel-pouts of
the same size, and eels of great size and excellence.

   In the lakes above Niagara Falls, we find no sturgeon, but this is replaced by the white fish, which is
very abundant and fine flavored, and a kind of herring
more delicate than that from the sea.   When this
country becomes better inhabited by the Europeans,
its fisheries will become a very considerable branch of
commerce.   For all these fisheries the Indians use a
dart, composed of two pieces of iron ten or twelve
inches long, pointed, and with two reversed barbs as
in a fish-hook, but not so large in proportion.   They
adjust these two pieces of iron to the end of a pole ten
or twelve feet long or over, and a quarter of an inch
apart.   They watch in the narrow places or in the
rapids for the fish as they are passing, and spear them.
It is seldom that they miss their aim.   They fish also
at night in their canoes.   They build a fire therein of cedar chips, and one man stands up in front with

his spear, while another behind with his paddle guides the canoe along the bank where the fish come to play in the light. He then spears them, and a fish ten feet under water, and as thick as an arm, could scarcely escape them.

In summer, the Indians are quite fond of hunting the deer, as this animal is persecuted by gnats, musketoes, which we call *cousins*, and brûlots, an insect almost imperceptible, with which the woods are filled, and seeks along the streams for places which have a clay bottom, where he jumps in to cover himself as a protection against these torments. The Indians know these places, and lie in wait, in concealment, where they can shoot several in a day. If they give chase in the woods, they have no need of dogs. The snow is favorable on account of the tracks which are left. At other seasons when the leaves are a little damp, and do not make a noise when they walk, the time is most favorable. An Indian recognizes at once the foot of the animal, upon the trodden ground or upturned leaves, and judges whether he is far off or near. He follows the track carefully, looking constantly to the right or left to perceive it, and sometimes he imitates the cry of the fawn. As soon as he perceives it, he stops, and only moves as the animal resumes its feeding. If it raises its head, the hunter remains in a fixed attitude in which he happens to be, and when he has come near enough he fires. If he has wounded his game, he shows an extraordinary sagacity in following

27

the trail of blood, and he very rarely returns without
bringing his prey.

When the Indians are in the vicinity of Europeans,
they trade with them for the surplus beyond their own
wants. To preserve the flesh of the deer which they
lay up, they take off the ribs and smoke it, after which
they roll it up like a piece of leather, and cut off morsels
as they wish. When they have no fresh meat, this is
not bad. They always save the brains of the deer, to
prepare their skins with, and which softens them as
perfectly as our tanner's preparations. To prevent
them from getting hard after they have been wet, they
smoke them. This operation is performed by collecting rotten wood, setting up pieces of dead wood around
it, in the form of a cone, and covering these with the
skins. They then put fire underneath, which gives
much smoke which the skins absorb in every part, and
then to get rid of the odor and dirt of the smoke, they
wash them. They thus render them very white and
pliant, and they do not harden any more than our skins
prepared in oil. They preserve the fat of the bears in
vessels, because this grease does not harden, at least
until it is mixed with that of the deer. In fineness, it
is much superior to goose oil, and it might even serve
as a salad, being better than butter.

They find in the woods in May and June, some pot
herbs such as little leeks that are very good, and gar-
licks sweeter and larger than ours. They are pear-
shaped, and the Europeans use them with success as a

remedy against scurvy, which the Indians do not know among themselves[1] any more than the gout or the rheumatism, although they are always sleeping upon the ground in the rain and dampness.

In the fall, the Indians eat walnuts and chesnuts, but as the trees which bear these are usually from sixty to ninety feet high, of smooth trunk without branches, and would be very difficult to climb, they cut them down to gather the fruit. They boil the walnuts in kettles, and extract the oil for their use. Into these kettles they like to put all kinds of meat, mingled with bruised Indian corn, which they eat without taking it from the fire. When they are thirsty, they dip up a dipper full of the broth, and they rarely drink pure water. They scarcely have any regular hour for their meals, which are taken by day or by night as they have an appetite, and they seldom use salt, although they have that which is very good.

We have not yet spoken of the most abundant kind of hunting in America, that of pigeons, to which the French have given the name of *tourtes*. The quantities that there appear from the month of May to September would appear fabulous. They pass upon the wing two or three hours at a time, and so thick that they make it dark, and this will last a whole day at a time. They do not take the trouble to shoot them with a gun,

---

[1] They eat nothing raw as we do, but always cook their herbs. — *Note in Original.*

but they kill them with a long pole at the end of which some leaves are left. It may happen that a single person may in this way kill some hundreds. They make their nests in the woods, which they cover over a space of four leagues in length by half a league in breadth. Whenever an Indian gives notice in his village that he has found a nesting place, they present him with an equipment for his good news, and the whole village go into the woods, men, women and children, and establish themselves there to eat the eggs and young pigeons during the whole time that the brooding lasts. This happens twice in a year, and we see no diminution in their numbers.[1]

The Indians travel upon foot or in canoes. Their foot journeys in summer are always short. The Iroquois and those who live along the Ohio, have some horses which they have stolen from the English who were pasturing them in the woods. The number is considerable, but they raise none. In their journeys on foot, every one carries his pack, which contains all the implements of the family, and from which a strap passes over the shoulders of the men, but the foreheads of the women on account of their breasts. They encamp early. The women and children make a cabin of boughs and build a fire, while the men go out to hunt to get something for supper. If the success is not

[1] These " pigeon roosts " are usually in beech woods, and are still of annual occurrence in Canada and northern New York. — ED.

good, they remain at least till they get some little provision, and live thus from day to day. An Indian will often set off alone to go sixty or a hundred leagues into the woods, with nothing but his gun, some powder and lead, a steel, a knife, his tomahawk, and a little kettle. When the Indians have some stream to pass, they make little rafts, with sticks of light wood, fastened together with wythes, and with an oar which they construct, or a long pole. They station themselves upright at one end, and thus cross rivers as large as the Rhone and the Rhine.

Foot journeys are more fatiguing on account of the swamps and low grounds full of water, which are always encumbered by the fallen pines or cedars. These are often found a quarter or half a league wide, and they seldom go through them except to make war. Although the season is more vigorous in winter, they then, nevertheless, have the advantage of finding the rivers frozen, and the woods full of snow, which covers their abattises. By the aid of their snow shoes, which are less inconvenient than at first appears when not accustomed to them, they overcome all these difficulties. These snow shoes are four or five feet long, and for about two feet in their widest part, they are woven with strips of hide. They pass the toe at about two-thirds from the hinder part, into a cavity formed by thongs passed behind the heel and over the foot, and so adjusted that the heel can be raised a little. It is necessary to walk with the feet thrown

outward, or otherwise they would interfere. If they
fall, they have great difficulty in getting up again.
The Indians have no fear of this, as the elasticity of
the snow shoes throws them forward, relieves the
fatigue of walking, and compensates for their inconvenience. They do not sink more than four or five
inches, into the lightest snows. They also make
sledges to carry their equipages very conveniently.
These are two flat strips of some hard and flexible
wood, ten or twelve feet long, and serve to make a
kind of sled a foot or a foot and a half wide, with the
floor made of birch bark or elm wood, and turned up
in front in a curve, so as to overcome the snow. They
fasten on them their articles, and with a strap passed
over their shoulders, draw them after them, or they
are drawn by a dog. This sled will carry eighty
pounds.

They encamp at an early hour in the thickets, and
construct a shelter on the side towards the wind, by
forming a half-roof with two crotches supporting little
poles covered with branches of spruce, flat foliage, or
rushes gathered from the swamps. Before their
shelter they build a good fire. This arrangement,
simple as is is, is preferable to a tent or shelter pit, in
which they might freeze, as they would then have no
communication with the fire. In their journeys they
take precaution against the cold. Their shoes, although only a simple prepared skin, are very warm,
and the snow is so dry that it does not wet. They

wrap their feet with pieces of blanket, and the sides of the shoes form a half boot which prevents the snow from getting in, while their feet would freeze with European shoes, as many have unhappily proved. The Indians fasten their blankets below with their belt, and make them pass over the head like a monk's hood, arranging them so well that they only expose their nose and hands. They make mittens of skins or flannel, hung to their neck by a string, which serves them better than gloves, because the separated fingers would be more liable to freeze. They make bonnets of a square of cloth, which they sew together at the side, well covering the neck and ears. We go into these details, because a similar arrangement would be good for troops who are obliged to march in winter, and would enable them to avoid many of the discomforts of the soldiers. If they find that some part of the neck or body has been frozen, which they at once know by its whiteness, they take snow and rub it until the blood resumes its circulation. They take care not to come near the fire, for if the part should thaw by the heat, it would turn into gangrene. The greatest inconvenience in these journeys, is in the spring, when the reflection of the sun's rays upon the snow or ice, makes them lose their sight[1] for some days, with very

[1] In speaking of the return of the French army from an attempt to surprise Fort William Henry in March, 1757, Garneau says:

" Their retreat was marked by an event which was repeated in Bonaparte's army in Egypt, but from a somewhat different cause

severe pain, on account of the inflammation which it
causes in the eyes, and for which there is no other
remedy except in the use of goggles of colored glass.

Canoes of elm bark are not used for long voyages,
as they are very frail. When the Indians wish to
make a canoe of elm bark, they select the trunk of a
tree which is very smooth, at the time when the sap
remains. They cut it around, above and below,
about ten, twelve or fifteen feet apart, according to the
number of people which it is to carry. After having
taken off the whole in one piece, they shave off the
roughest of the bark, which they make the inside of
the canoe. They make end ties of the thickness of a
finger, and of sufficient length for the canoe, using
young oaks or other flexible and strong wood, and
fasten the two larger folds of the bark between these
strips, spreading them apart with wooden bows which
are fastened in about two feet apart. They sew up
the two ends of the bark with strips drawn from the
inner bark of the elm, giving attention to raise up a
little the two extremities, which they call *pinces*, making a swell in the middle, and a curve on the sides, to
resist the wind. If there are any chinks, they sew
them together with thongs, and cover them with chewing gum which they crowd in by heating it with a coal

The dazzling whiteness of the snow, struck a third of the detachment
with a kind of ophthalmia, so that they were obliged to be led by the
hand the rest of the way. But two days after their return, all the
sick had recovered their sight by the aid of simple remedies."— iii, p.
88.— ED.

of fire. The bark is fastened to the wooden bows by thongs. They add a mast, made of a piece of wood, and cross piece to serve as a yard, and their blankets serve them as sails. These canoes will carry from three to nine persons and all their equipage. In these frail vessels they sometimes undertake voyages upon the lakes of a dozen leagues. They sit upon their heels without moving, as do also their children when they are in, from fear of losing their balance when the whole machine would upset; but this very seldom happens unless struck by a flaw of wind. Their paddles are four or five feet long. The sight of such a craft, which is only three or four inches out of the water, would surely frighten a European. If the canoe overturns, they turn it right by swimming, and then get in at one of the ends. When they land, they take great pains not to allow it to strike, by which it would be broken. They carry it on shore, and again put it afloat, when they embark. They use these vessels particularly in their war parties. They make them everywhere that they have occasion to go up or down rivers.

The canoes made of birch bark, are much more solid and more artistically constructed. The frame of these canoes is made of strips of cedar wood, which is very flexible, and which they render as thin as a side of a sword scabbard, and three or four inches wide. They all touch one another, and come up to a point between the two end strips. This frame is covered with the bark of the birch tree sewed together like skins,

28

secured between the end strips, and tied along the ribs
with the inner bark of the roots of the cedar, as we
twist willows around the hoops of a cask. All these
seams are covered with chewing gum, as is done with
canoes of elm bark. They then put in cross bars to
hold it and to serve as seats, and a long pole, which
they lay on from fore to aft in rough weather to prevent it from being broken by the shocks occasioned by
pitching. They have them with three, six, twelve and
even twenty-four places, which are designated as so many
seats. The French are almost the only people who use
these canoes for their long voyages. They will carry
as much as three thousand pounds. Four men will
carry them in their portages, and two men will commonly be able to lift them. These little crafts will
endure gales of wind that would trouble vessels. They
have only to take care that they do not strike. If they
happen to get holes, they close them carefully with
pieces of bark which they carry with them. These
boats also serve as a cabin, as they turn them up on
the side and place them on one or two paddles, and lie
down underneath sheltered from the wind. This is the
ordinary cabin upon journeys and in hunting.

If man was created to be lord of the earth, this is
nowhere more true than in this part of the world,
where he is only subject to his own will. Without
restraint of law, and able to satisfy all his wants, and
and these but few, he appears to be indeed free. To
their misfortune we came among them, and we have

taught them to use our cloths for their garments. They cannot now go and get powder and brandy, without which the greater part will perish. This necessity made them remain tranquil towards the English whom they did not love but despised, because their traders sought to cheat them. The Indians formerly had usages and utensils to which they are now scarcely accustomed. They made pottery, drew fire from wood, and their arrows furnished them with food. They made needles and fish hooks of fish-bones. The tendons of animals served them as thread, which they divided and drew into threads as fine as they wanted. Their women were skillful and industrious in making and fitting their garments.

When the Indian has enough to eat, his wants are satisfied, and he thinks only of enjoying himself by smoking or sleeping, without giving a thought for the morrow. Unless something arouses his ideas he thinks of nothing, and exhibits an extreme tranquility and patience which makes him appear melancholy. The habit of being alone and isolated, may tend to this, but it is so strong in the Indian's nature, that if treated in the best manner, and lodged superbly, he would grow weary within a month, and perish if he could not run in the woods, and lead his accustomed life, as has been actually proved. His only thoughts are of the chase, and of his country's enemies, and he is only occupied with the means of maintaining himself tranquil upon his mat, that is to say, in his country. He has no proper idea of what we call *ambition*, and can never covet what belongs to another, his only aspiration being to be thought a great hunter or a formidable man, who has killed many people. If a European undertakes to recount the power of the king of France or of England, he listens very attentively to what they say, and then will ask very coolly: "Is he a good hunter?—has he killed many enemies?" If they assure him that he has been to war, and that he fires well, "Oh!" he cries, "That's the man!" This is the highest praise that the Indian could bestow.

They are very hospitable. If one enters their cabin, they may all take from their kettle and eat without having anything to return. They offer you their best, and even deprive themselves of their necessaries of life to give to a stranger. This is reciprocated, and they imagine that they can refuse nothing. Among some nations, they even offer you their wives, so as not to be lonesome.

They think that the Master of Life, having created them in the land they inhabit, no one has a right to trouble them in their possessions. As they recognize no territorial property, they think that all their country belongs to them in common, and that the land where they live, and where the bones and spirits of their ancestors are, is sacred and inviolable. They think they cannot leave it, without going to take some other tract which should be their hunting ground. This sentiment born with them, renders them very delicate upon this subject, and it is constantly an occasion for war, when one nation comes to hunt around the houses of another. The traveling Indians even take care to leave the skins of animals that that they kill upon the territory of a foreign nation, hung upon the trees, so that they can have the profit of them. It was therefore, quite out of place for the English to say, that they had bought of some one among them several countries. Europeans were only tolerated in early times, because they first made presents, and as being useful, and possessing all they could desire which they came and offered them, to draw them from their misery and to supply their wants. Upon this sole title they received them, and they then offered to sustain them against the nations with which they were at war, from which they were regarded as benefactors and friends. But when the Europeans came in force, they obliged the Indians to cede such lands as they needed. The latter found themselves too much straightened in their hunting, and retired into the interior, and were forced to seek an asylum among other nations who received them with charity, and incorporated them among themselves. Since this time they have preserved, especially among the Loups on the Ohio River, a hostility which has been shown towards the English every time they could find a chance.[1]

---

[1] It was they that raised in 1763-4, almost all the tribes beyond the Alleghanies against the English, and made a cruel war. — *Note in Original.*

The French only occupied the banks of the St. Lawrence, and had not hitherto crowded the Indians, who still retained the whole of the interior of the country. They endeavored on the contrary to preserve them as much as possible, by the establishment of Christian villages. Besides the advantage of propagating Christianity, this idea was a good one, because the welfare, that the benevolence of the king caused them to enjoy, attracted to us their friendship and esteem. The English now very much regret that they did not manage thus in the beginning of their establishments.

The Indians regard as their chiefs the oldest members of the first branch of their nations. Some of them enjoy a little more authority than others, and they will go so far as to allow themselves to be struck by them without seeking revenge, but this is very uncommon. Such is the nation of Loups at Theaogen. Every right of preëminence is reduced to this, and whatever is gained beyond, is through insinuation or exhortation. If any one does not wish to do as they say, they have no means of compelling them. The chief only serves them as a point of reunion, for their councils or deliberations, and it is in his name that the nation speaks in public affairs. The youth show a very exemplary respect and deference towards their parents and the aged, which leads them to attend very willingly to all they say or hint to them. They obey them without a murmur, and are held in check without complaint. In their journeys, the young people undertake with out a word, the care of making the cabins, and go to look up wood while the od peolple are quietly smoking.

No ideas of metaphysics or morals ever entered the heads of the Indians, and they believe whatever is told them upon these subjects, without having a very strong impression. They say they have not enough spirit to comprehend things which are only subjects of reasoning. From this we may imagine that they make very poor Christians. When a missionary speaks to them of the Trinity, or the Incarnation of the Word, they quietly reply: These things are good for you who have enough spirit, but we have not enough to be persuaded; we believe it because you say so. They compare the Trinity to a piece of pork, where we find the lean meat, the fat and the rind, three distinct parts that form the same piece. The missionaries have persuaded them[1] that Judas had red hair, and that the English who have generally this kind of hair, are of his race, and this is a reason for their greater dislike to them.

The king having sent over with the first colonists, some priests of the foreign missions, Sulpicians, Recollects and Jesuits, these missionaries attended as much as they could in all the treaties, and invited the Indians to come and settle in the places which they designated, where they could be lodged, fed and clothed, and be

---

[1] The author very improperly attributes to the missionaries in general, a remark perhaps made by some one of them, or by one of the *coureurs de bois.* — *Note in Original.*

supplied with all their wants. Many, through laziness, became so familiar as to come and profit by this benevolence, and voluntarily submitted themselves to become instruments. If nothing had been given them, and if they had not found a decided advantage in adopting this course, we should have had but few, as we may infer from the small numbers that we have attracted notwithstanding all the amenities they have received. Their indifference in believing or not believing, further determines them, as also promises for the life to come. Their children brought up in the Christian religion, follow the example of their parents, at least until their passions lead them to abandon the missions, which is happening constantly. Those who remain, follow with much decency the ceremonies of religion.

It is very edifying to see them in church, the men on one side, and women on the other, always upon their knees, with a more devout air than any capuchin, never speaking to one another, and never turning their heads. The women, much enveloped in their blankets, sing with the men in two choruses, the prayers of the church, which the missionaries have translated for them, and which they commit to memory. Their songs are very sweet and harmonious, and we never hear any discord as in our villages. In regard to the sacraments, they use them as much as their missionaries desire, and yield readily to the public and private penances which they impose, in which they somewhat recall the rules of the primitive church. The Indians pay exactly the tenth part of their corn and peltries, to which the missionaries have accustomed them.

Drunkenness, is not, however, a vice less prevalent among these new converts. The obligation of taking care of women they do not love, is the only thing that wearies them, so that many abandon the missions to return to their villages, so that they can live in freedom. We may say in general, that they have acquired a little humanity, and a particular attachment for the French, as being of the same religion or prayers, because they make a difference between the catholic religion and the religion of the English. The priests have taken care to persuade them, that the latter is almost no Christianity. If the Indians who have embraced our faith have become more humane, we should confess that while they have had more communication with us, they have also been infected by our vices more than others who have been less exposed to the contagion.

All these statements are exactly true, and it is a shame that they scarcely agree with exaggerated accounts of the missionaries. The small number of Indians who have been converted, during the hundred and eighty years since we have occupied this vast continent, is a proof of their indifference to religion. They may preach what they will, they listen quietly and without emotion, and always return to their common avocations, having not enough spirit to believe and follow what is told them.

Their priests live like them, and adopt their manner of life. Although they have killed some priests, it was never because they hated their dogmas, but because they regarded them as belonging to a hostile nation.

We have noticed that the king bore all the expense of the missions. When the Indians have found themselves ill at ease on account of two great clearings, they have asked to be removed to more distant localities. The king has borne the expense of these new establishments, and the missionaries have ceded their old villages to the Europeans, reserving to themselves the seigniorial rights. In this way they have acquired in Canada the property of eight out of ten villages. The whole island of Montreal, and the city of that name, has also come into the possession of the Sulpicians.

There are now no nations known, who have not heard our religion spoken of, and many have even come to witness its ceremonies, which they all respect in their way. The Indians have a kind of reverence for our priests, whom they call *Praying Fathers*, because they think from their manners, and from the discourses which they hold, that they are men entirely occupied in praying to the Supreme Being.

These natives of America, have no very distinct idea of this Infinite Being; they render to him no homage, and only designate him as the MASTER OF LIFE. They believe that all events depend upon him, and that they cannot succeed in any enterprise without his favor. In their discourses they regard themselves as subjects of fate. They believe that there are bad spirits which cause sinister events, and every thing which appears to them extraordinary. They give these the name of *Manitous*. The sea, the lakes, the rivers and everything created, have their manitous, that is, evil-doing spirits, to whom they make offerings or sacrifices. If they are struck by a flaw of wind upon a lake, and find themselves in peril, they throw overboard their tobacco, or some implement or utensil to appease the Manitou of the Lake, and they do the same when passing a dangerous rapid. When they are going out for hunting or war, to ensure success they make a kind of sacrifice, which consists in erecting a post to which they suspend a dog or some other animal which they have killed, some feathers, some tobacco, or whatever else comes into their mind. This is about all that the ceremonies of their religion amount to. They are very superstitious. Any thing that appears to them of bad augury will break up a war party even after they have traveled some hundreds of leagues, and when they are ready to strike; and it is the same in hunting or any other enterprise. They call praying, *practicing medicine.*

The custom of being alone, gives them a habit of revery. That which they call *juggling*, is as follows: A man or a woman finding himself or herself of this disposition, wraps up in a blanket and thus remains a very long time. Their imagination is heated, and an enthusiasm seizing them, they believe that they see future events, and announce them with confidence. In fact their prophesy often amounts to nothing, but more than once it has come to pass. The Europeans who have been among them relate upon this subject some supernatural things.

We will here give two facts well known in the French army :

In 1756, M. Duplessis, commandant at Niagara, sent a party of twenty-five Missisakes to Oswego, while the women remained near the fort. They assembled every evening to " make medicine," one old woman singing, while the others replied in chorus. The officers went to see the ceremony. At the end of six or seven days, they enquired why they made no more medicine, when an old woman replied that their people had beaten : that she had juggled and that they had killed many people. An officer who knew these juggleries, wrote down upon the spot, the day that she designated, and when the party returned, he questioned the Indians and prisoners whose answers confirmed the old woman's account. It is at least sixty leagues from Niagara to Oswego, and no person had come either by land or water. The Indians had lost two men, took twelve scalps, and led away three ship carpenters as prisoners.

In 1758, about the month of March, M. de Vaudreuil sent a large party of domiciliated Indians to Carillon. These Indians upon arriving at the fort,

went to the commandant and asked him to give them
some provisions, as they wished to rest some days before going to Fort George. After returning to their
camp, one of them juggled, and informed that the
English were very near Fort Carillon, and that he
should at once go and attack them. The rest trusted
to this inspiration, and went back to the commandant's
quarters to notify him that they wanted to depart the
next day, counting upon finding a party of the English.
The commandant although astonished at this idea, was
quite willing to get rid of them, and several officers
and soldiers volunteered to be of the party. Before
they had gone three leagues, they met the tracks of the
English upon the lake which was then frozen, coming
from the direction of Carillon. They followed these
tracks and when their scouts came to the top of a
hillock in the woods, the English were going down
into a valley which was between them, to the number
of two hundred and fifty. These scouts notified their
party, who soon engaged the enemy, attacking them
just as they began to come out of the valley. But
eight of them escaped. They were all volunteers, with
their officers, under the orders of Robert Rogers. All
the rest were killed, and they took few prisoners.[1]

In almost every village they have jugglers by pro-
fession, who are also doctors, or rather real charlatans.
They shut themselves up alone in a cabin, where they

See volume i. p. 100, of this work.— Ed.

act like persons possessed, and when they come out
they deal out their prophesies. This is commonly upon the fate of a sick person, or upon the luck of a war
or hunting party. In the former case they will say
that the Maniton of the disease demands a feast, the
result of which is that he will get drunk, and then he
will give a remedy. If it has a bad effect, the self-
styled doctor is sometimes well beaten or even killed,
because the Indians are offended at having been duped.
Each family has its particular remedies, but these
jugglers have nothing that is very good. They have
knowledge of some excellent plants, especially for
wounds. It is at least certain that when they have any
broken bones, no surgeon could treat them more
surely, with less style or with greater promptness.
They are acquainted with a great number of plants,
roots and barks of trees, which they employ very usefully. Since Europeans have been in America, they
have not sufficiently endeavored to induce them to
show these remedies, which might be of great use in
our medicines. It is true the Indians are very jealous
in retaining their recipes among themselves, but with
time and presents, we might be able in the end to ob-
tain their secrets. They cure themselves of the most
stubborn cases of venereal disease without mercury.
They have a root which comes larger than a turnip,
and which will bring to suppuration inward abscesses.
It reproduces itself from suckers, and grows in damp
and somewhat marshy localities.

With other plants they heal cuts,[1] as quickly as the best balm. They call it anise, and its flavor is excellent. The diseases to which they are most subject, are pleurisies, discharges from the chest, and consumptions caused by the large quantities of brandy which they drink. Although they love to preserve their lives, we may say that there are no classes of men who fear death less, as they regard it as a pathway to another life. When they feel themselves near their end, they sing the death song, until they can speak no longer. This song is a kind of lamentation, which each one makes according to his own fancy, but always in the same tone.

When an Indian is dead, we hear no cry nor plaint in the cabin, but they come to make their farewell visit. They bury them with all their finest garments, their arms, and a keg of brandy to help them on their journey. They raise over the grave a kind of cabin made of poles in the form of a monument, and by its side another great post on which are fixed the family arms. They mark thereon some characters representing the number of scalps and prisoners they have taken. Some nations have the custom of sending the women during the first eight days, to build a little fire near the grave, and to sit upon their heels, remaining there immovable for a quarter to half an hour at a time. If he dies while hunting, even if it has been

---

[1] The plant with which they heal themselves is called by Charlevoix, *Plante Universelle*. Its leaves when boiled, heal all kinds of wounds. These leaves are of the breadth of a hand, and have the form of those of the fleur de lys.— *Note in Original*.

three or four months they will disinter him and carry him in their canoes to bury him in their villages. They do the same in regard to their children.

At the end of a year, they come to hold an anniversary which consists of a feast near the tomb. They then disinter the keg of brandy and drink it. They believe that after death, the soul goes to a great country beyond the sea, which they term the great lake. They think that there they will find whatever they wish to hunt at will, and only for amusement, and that their only occupation will be in dancing.

They have no tradition which preserves the least idea of their origin, and all that they say has been suggested to them by Europeans. There are those who believe that a woman came down from the heavens upon the waters, and that having put her foot upon a turtle to rest herself, the earth was formed around this turtle, and that this woman gave birth to the human race.[1] As they have adopted for their armorial bearings, some the bear, others a turtle, a wolf, a fox, &c., they designate their families by the names of these animals, and think themselves descendants from them.[2]

---

[1] This idea appears to have come originally from the Asiatic Indians, who communicated it to the islands of Japan, from whence this fable passed to America. — *Note in Original*.

This idea of the origin of the Indian race, is more fully given by Nicholas Cusick, a Tuscarora, in a tract published about forty years since. See also *Dwight's Travels* and the writings of Henry R. Schoolcraft. — ED.

[2] The Baron de la Hontan found in this usage the puerile rules of our vain science of heraldry. — *Note in Original*.

Some think that they came out of the ground that they inhabit. As they have no writing, they designate themselves by the figures of these animals, which they draw upon bark, or the trunks of trees. They will carve these figures in a style that would do credit to our ordinary workmen. They use in making these figures, which are very expressive, a crooked knife, the same that they work with in carving out their wooden utensils.

When a family take to mourning for one of its members, they quit all their ornaments, and go dressed as simply as possible, and mark themselves only in black. This mourning lasts about a year. The relatives, friends and those interested in this family, make presents to cover the dead, which consists in giving them a belt or a garment. They replace the dead in their cabins by a scalp or a prisoner, and they do not quit mourning until this latter ceremony, which is one of the principal causes of their wars, being always obliged to have at least one nation from whom others can take prisoners or scalps to replace their dead.

All the nations in the eastern part of America, although they have nearly the same language, are not so allied among themselves, but that they make war with one another, of which an enumeration has been given by English and French authors. The English found them in this condition when they began to settle these countries, and it favored the establishment of their colonies. But their common misfortunes have reunited the Indians. These nations have had many considerable wars to sustain against the Iroquois, who had sent them the *machicote*, that is to say, according to their language, had forbidden them from bearing arms, and regarded them as women.

The Iroquois are six nations united together, including the Tuscaroras, who had been almost destroyed, and whom they have incorporated among them, as also the Erie or Cat nation, of whom but a few individuals remain, who have been adopted by the Senecas. The Iroquois nation is the most perfectly allied of all those in America, and forms a true federated republic. This union has given them a decided superiority over all the other nations who being less numerous, were broken and unable to escape them. The Iroquois went to seek their enemies with thousands of warriors, as far as to the rivers which fall into the Mississippi, and to the shores of Lake Superior. All of these incursions never ended without the death or capture of men, and the destruction of these nations. This is what the Indians call *eating them*. They never had a thought of extending their country, nor of gaining a larger hunting ground, nor of subjugating other nations to themselves. This is proved by the fact that notwithstanding all the advantages they enjoyed over the different nations they have almost destroyed, such as the Hurons, the Nepicins and the Algonquins, who were formerly very numerous, the Iroquois have never sought to take the lands of these nations, nor to reduce them to slavery.

The claims of the English were therefore very frivolous, when they supposed that by virtue of their pretended alliance with the Iroquois, that they had rights in the countries of all those nations with whom these people had been at war, and whom they had subjugated. These nations may have diminished, but they have never changed the condition of their various cantons.

The Outaouais, the Sauteurs or Ochibois and the Missisakes, who have almost the same language, and who are allied among themselves, although very near the Iroquois, have sustained themselves against them, on account of this union. The other nations more distant and less united, have, in the meantime, suffered somewhat. They are not even confederated for hunting, and therefore could not fight with success against the vast armies of the Iroquois which amounted they say to twenty thousand men. If such armies had existed, it is certain that they would have destroyed all the nations through which they might pass.

When the French came to America, they landed upon the shores of the Algonquins, one of the most ancient nations upon the continent, as we may judge from the extent of their language, and upon those of the Nepicius and Hurons who were at war with the Iroquois. The French having taken part against these latter, they became thus the natural enemies of their establishments. They came near dislodging us from the Island of Montreal, and the plains east of the river St. Lawrence where they came to hunt, as we have done them considerable harm in the early period of the colony.[1] They were always urged on, first by the solicitations of Swedes and Dutch who formed settlements upon the Hudson river, and then by the English who succeeded them. This gave us an opportunity to ally ourselves more intimately with all the nations of the continent, because they all dreaded the Iroquois, and we were always ready to sustain them or to make alliances with them against the common enemy.

As for the rest, the French did not usually meet the Indians except at their posts, where they supplied them with whatever would satisfy their wants, and had become necessary for them. When they have had any difficulty with any of these nations, they have taken care to always unite themselves with the others against them, and have soon obliged them to remain quiet, because the Indians distrust one another much more if they are supposed to have relations with Europeans.

The Indian nations find themselves sometimes entangled with one another, either upon returning from the chase, or in their reciprocal embassies when they pass their time in festivities, or rather debaucheries with brandy. They often take precautions at such times so that no harm shall happen. The women try to hide the arms of their husbands as much as possible,

---

[1] They have many times brought us within two fingers' breadth of ruin. See the *Hist. de la Nouvelle France* by Father Charlevoix.— *Note in Original.*

for they never drink without treating all the rest. At their festivals they all eat till almost ready to burst. Their feasts often consist in drinking, and where eating is out of the question. Ten or a dozen Indians will drink as many as fifteen or twenty pots of brandy, and more in the same proportion. The youngest is charged with pouring the drink, and each one in his turn drinks the same quantity. The one who distributes, keeps so good an account, that his portion is always found equal to that of the others. The women who do not care much about drink take their portion, put it in the mouth and at once throw it into a little kettle. They then sell it back to the revellers when their brandy is gone.

The Indians have so great a passion for this drink, that when once they have been led to taste, they will deprive themselves generally of all that they have, to swallow more. We may imagine what an uproar and confusion this will occasion. They begin by singing, and then follow with the most vehement yells. They reserve for these drunken revels, to make their reproaches and to quarrel, which is always upon the want of bravery.[1] These quarrels, almost always end in the death of some one, or cost them at least some torn ears. If they attack a man who is not drunk, and who has not the prudence to steal away at an early hour, he often becomes a victim, because it

---

[1] If a man is wounded by a gun shot, or a sharp weapon, it is deemed a death that demands vengeance.—*Note in Original.*

would be dishonorable for him to strike a man in a
state of drunkenness, as they say that then they have
no spirit. If he goes off then, he fears the other will
reproach him for having fled. In this alternative, to
show his courage he will tell them to strike, and the
others may kill him. By such accidents good and
brave Indians have been killed.

If the man killed is of the same nation as that of
the slayer they say nothing at the time, but bring it
up on some other drunken occasion. If the latter is
found there, as seldom fails to happen, because they
cannot resist the temptation to drink, some one of the
relatives of the deceased kill him. Some of them
pretend to more drunkenness than is real, so as better
to execute their design. In any other condition they
would not dare to undertake their revenge, because
they could not then excuse themselves by saying that
they had no courage. Finally to remedy these succes-
sive hostilities, the relatives of the murderer cover the
dead body, as we have described, and this gives occasion for another war party to go and seek to replace
him. This measure does not always restrain the
mother or wife of the dead, from mourning his loss,
or from their employing some one to slay the assassin.
We may judge what destruction of human life these
accidents involve. If the latter has killed several, the
nation willingly consents that he shall die at a festival
prepared on purpose, at which even his father attends.
When the Europeans wish to exhort them to desist

from such designs, they quietly answer that he should die, because he is of no value.

If such an event should happen between different nations, it becomes much more furious. The whole nation is insulted and obliged to avenge the death. If the nation of the murderer wish to avoid war, it is necessary for it to deliver him up so that they can cover the dead, but even then they are not always contented. The parties injured wish to take their revenge, even a long time afterwards, and these quarrels sometimes only end by the destruction of one or the other, or until other nations interpose their authority. The more injury that is done to an Indian tribe, the more they become intractable, and they can only in the end become conciliated, except by gentle measures.

In their embassies between nations to speak of peace, alliance, or some other political object, the deputation is always numerous, and is composed of chiefs or elders of the nation, the war chiefs and young warriors, and they have with them an orator. Some are found in almost all the villages. They are commonly the best talkers. They carry with them belts of white wampum, upon which is represented the subject of the embassy. If it is an alliance, they picture out some cabins which designate their villages, and trace a road from one village to another, and Indians holding each other by the hand. We may easily infer the meaning of what they would wish to say. The more important the business, the larger become these belts. They carry a calumet of peace with them, which is a pipe made of marble, or some other soft stone, red, brown or black, of which the grain is very fine, and which they can work out with a knife. They fit in a wooden tube two or three feet long. This wood which is very hard, has a thick pith, which they take out with a brass wire heated red in the fire. It is painted yellow and black, in a flaming design, or covered with a braid of white, yellow, red or black porcupine quills, with a row of eagle's feathers attached by a cord of porcupine quills and pendant ribbons of different colors, which give a very pleasing effect.

The cortege having arrived at the chief's cabin, all those who compose it, sit down upon the ground without saying a word, and light the calumet. The chief begins to smoke, and then he presents it to the chief of the nation with whom they have come to negotiate, and the calumet passes from one to another, and they each smoke a puff. This is the strongest mark of peace and amity that they can give. If they cannot agree they refuse to smoke. After this ceremony the orator arises, relates his journey, says they are much fatigued, and ends by indicating the day when they intend to depart. If they are friends, they send them something to eat, and they all retire together to cabin themselves without saying more.

On the appointed day they come to the council, and the orator delivers what he has to say to them, giving strings or belts according to importance of what he has

to propose. They remain so still that one could hear
a fly buzz, and all with their pipes between their teeth,
as is also sometimes that of the orator. At the important passages, the deputies approve the discourse by a
ho ho. The others do not reply the same day, but only
indicate when they will. With same ceremonies the
orator of the nation replies to everything, repeating
article by article, and giving belts or strings for each
subject. The council being finished, they separate and
then begin the dances and festivals among them which
last till their departure.

If they wish to engage a nation in war, they carry
belts of black wampum, with their hatchets painted
above, in red, with vermilion. The larger it is, the
more pressing the invitation. This is their custom of
offering the hatchet.

The calumet dance, which is one of their greatest
ceremonies, is never held but in case of agreement.
All the Indians sit in a circle, with their hatchets or
tomahawks, and knives in their hands. Some have
only *chichiquois*, which are gourds filled with little
pebbles, or the hoofs from the feet of deer fastened
together at the end of a handle. They also have a
kettle drum made of a kettle covered with a skin.
They select the most active for dancing, while another
sings an air proper for the dance. All these instruments are beaten in cadence, and the dancer with his
calumet in one hand and a chichiquois in the other, in
the middle of the ring, follows the air, keeping time

with regular but violent movements in every part of
his body. He stoops down almost to the ground, and
after making sundry contortions, rises quickly, making
various motions in the interval. He then renews the
dance in which he shows great dexterity and strength.
It has much regularity, and would not offend in a
theatre.

From what we have said we may well infer, that the
Indians have frequent occasion for war, as they must
always have some nation "to eat," and can never be
quiet without it. An Indian who should pass three
years without going to war, would not be reputed a
man, and would be assailed with reproaches in their
festivals.

When war is decided against a nation, there are not
found wanting war chiefs who seek to make up parties.
They choose one having the most reputation. He supplies himself with brandy and some equipments, and
invites the young people, and especially his relatives,
to a feast, which consisted in eating a dog, which they
have killed by flaying. The repast ended, they begin
to drink brandy. The war chief arises, sings the war
song, and each one in turn recounts all his exploits,
striking a post, and throwing down a pledge to confirm
the fact. He speaks of all the nations whose homes he
has attacked, and marks with his hatchet on the side
towards which they are situated. He announces his
intentions with the most menacing air possible, and
invites those who have courage to follow him. He ends

by throwing down a belt of black wampum painted in red, with disdain upon the earth, and invites those who have heart to take it up, announcing that he intends to give it to the one who shall show the greatest courage. All the young people sit in a circle around him, replying by a *hé hé* in cadence, which serves as the refrain of his song.

When this chief ends, the first who decides, rises up, and goes through the same ceremony, sings his war song, recounts his exploits, strikes the post, and throws down his pledges of assurance, and takes up the belt, still singing; — protests that he shall be found worthy of gaining it, and then throws it down. The others get up as they one by one decide, and go through the same ceremony. Those who do not wish to join the party, drink, but do not dance. The ceremony being ended, all those who are to form the party array themselves as warriors. They strip to the breech cloth and moccasins, and paint their whole bodies with reddish brown, in streaks which they make with their fingers, and cut their hair or rather pull it out by the roots, except the forelock. They ornament the head, and cover it with vermillion, and above they put a white tuft which is the mark they carry for war.

As soon as they are all assembled, they march together, their weapons in their hands, and dancing around go from cabin to cabin singing an air, of which the final words are *ha ha*, *he he*, *hen*, *hi hi*, &c., turning towards one another, knife in hand, and gesticulating violently. They make some little presents. During this time the young girls follow them, always dancing with a tossing motion, as when dancing in the evenings as we have related, and this is to those who treat them the best. This continues several days, and until the moment of departure. They put themselves then in file one after another, the chief at the head, preceded by the youngest who carries the medicine bag, in which is a bird or other animal, which each war chief takes for his Manitou. They have also in this bag some simples for wounds or sickness. They have a very great regard for this bag, which always precedes them on their marches. The war chief sings his parting song, which is a prayer to the Master of Life that he will favor them in their designs. Several girls follow the band, carrying the packages of the young men, and sometimes accompany them three or four days, when they return. They make their journeys in canoes, because the rivers are the only highways in the country.

The young people are charged as we have said with all extra duties, which they divide among themselves without a murmur. If some idle ones do not wish to do it, they make no reproach. If some one juggles and desires to return, he leaves without ceremony. They encamp early to hunt, as they carry no provisions and only their ammunition. They have, however, sometimes, a little sack of *sagamité*, which is some Indian corn pounded, scorched and cooked in a kettle with fat and maple sugar. They save this kind of food till the time when they are near the enemy, or for some occasion of scarcity. By mixing with water alone, it makes a very healthy food, and both nourishing and pleasant. Two hands full of this food will do for the subsistence of a day, if they apprehend a scarcity of food.

When they are in the enemy's country, they do not fire, and if they have no arrows, they live by fishing, or upon roots, or their sagamité. But whenever they are ready to strike, or when they flee, or after an action, they remain three or four days without eating. In approaching the frontier, where they might meet some one, they take care to seek the densest thickets, and to efface all their tracks where they enter them. They also conceal their canoes and all their packs and ornaments, paint their whole bodies black, and carry with them only their arms and their Manitou without forgetting their mirrors. They hold frequent councils to decide how they shall disperse after having struck, or where they shall rendezvous, &c. They never march without first sending out scouts a distance of two or three leagues around them, upon whose reports they act. Their sagacity in discovering every kind of trace is remarkable. The trodden earth, leaves upturned, or the dew brushed off, will not prevent them from recognizing the tracks of deer. They know the tracks of the Indians by the kind of shoes, but more especially by the manner in which the foot is put down or turned. They judge still more easily if they are Europeans, by the step and the sole of the shoe. They even distinguish an Englishman from a Frenchman, and ascertain very correctly how many people there are, as well by the tracks as by the fires that they build, and by their places of sleeping, if these traces are those of a party in a campaign. Those who are the first to discover are almost sure to beat the others. They will follow the track many days, until they find them in a position that gives them advantage, as in a cabin, or dispersed to sleep, or in a march where they are separated. They will conceal themselves near the place where they wish to strike, each one in the place assigned by the war chief, and remain quiet until he gives the signal by a cry made as he strikes the hand upon his mouth. He is answered by all the assailants, who are now all concealed, each with his prey selected. At the first moment of the enemy's surprise, they fire upon him, and it is seldom that they fail to bring some of them down. They issue out at once, hatchet in hand, to throw themselves upon them, and do not stop before they are all destroyed. If they think they are not much wounded, or that they are in a condition for defense, they give them a blow on the head with a hatchet. If they flee, they throw it after them, and plant it in their shoulders, in which they become very adroit. As soon as the man has fallen, they run to him, put their knee between his shoulders, take a lock of hair in one hand, and with their knife in the other give a blow separating the skin from the head, and tearing off a piece.

This is a thing quickly done; then showing the scalp they utter a cry which they call the death cry. During their combats, they raise cries as furious as possible, to animate one another and intimidate the enemy. If they do not see themselves pressed, and if the victory has cost them blood, they exercise great barbarities towards those they kill, or upon the bodies of the dead, whom they disembowel, and then paint themselves with their blood.

Although they repent much of these horrors, they nevertheless give way to them, to animate themselves for courage, and inspire a kind of fury, which makes them appear more brave among their fellows, and heedless of peril. They bind all the prisoners they can take with the belts which serve to carry their packets, and which they never quit. They tie them so strongly by the neck, arms and waist, that it is impossible for them to get free. If they fear to be attacked, they at once run and disperse to the rendezvous agreed upon, which is sometimes nine or ten leagues off, according to the country, and the circumstances in which they find themselves. They sometimes assign two to aid the prisoners in marching, taking them by the hands. If notwithstanding this they are unable to follow, they take off their scalps.

When they are in ambuscade near some village or fort, as there are commonly some clearings in the environs, they seek to approach in the night. If they do so by day, they lie with their belly to the ground, and cover their head and back with herbs, leaves or straw, according to the color of the ground where they are. They advance on their hands, pushing their guns before them until they are conveniently advanced. They judge according to their strength, whether the post is assailable or not, which is always decided to their advantage because the few whom they see exposed, they allow to pass them and watch with extreme patience the favorable moment and opportunity, especially if they are only two or three in number. Their purpose accomplished, they raise a cry as they retreat, and leave behind some mark to designate what nation has struck.

They scarcely amuse themselves by pillaging. If they have time they try to kill some animals for provisions. It is seldom that they burn houses, because they do not wish to be discovered. Their principal object is, to bring away prisoners, or to take scalps. When they find they cannot succeed, they do not fire. They embarrass themselves but little with their own traces, or the spoils of the dead. It is important to remark here, that if they have occasion to lead off many prisoners or take many scalps, they persevere until the operation is finished, but when the party amounts to three hundred and have taken only one or two scalps, they do not begin another operation doubting their power to ruin the country or to kill other men. They say that if they were not contented the Master of Life would be offended at them, and that they would run the risk of not succeeding, or of loosing their people. Thus they go to their homes, to touch the goal, if I may so express myself, and having traveled two or three hundred leagues, they make other parties and return. When they have returned to their rendezvous, they dispose of their prisoners according to the taste of their nation. If he is an European, they cut their hair in their fashion, and dress them like Indians. They secure them by night, and fasten them to some branches of trees by their feet and hands, in such a way that they cannot escape. They put around their neck a belt of wampum, such as our ladies wear, and paint them red, which is a mark of slavery. They take care to feed him of every thing that they have, so that he shall not pine away on the road. They stretch their scalps around a little hoop in the form of a drum head, with the hair hanging down one side. They grease them and sprinkle them with vermilion, as well as on the inside of the skin.

The war chief takes care to give the belt promised to him who was the first to go upon the enemy, or who has made the best blow, which they decide among themselves, equitably and without a murmur. If the chief has some equipment, of which some one is in want, he robs himself to give it to him. If it is by good conduct, bravery, good luck and liberality that he requires the reputation of being a good war chief. Although he should succeed in his hopes in an attack, if he should have the misfortune to lose some one, every

32

thing is plunged into sorrow, and the glory with which
he is covered is counted for nothing. They require
him to return to war, to avenge the blood of the deceased, and to replace him in the family. The Iroquois take great care to bring back all the wounded,
even when they may be of a foreign nation. This is
one of their first duties. They make a kind of litter,
or they pass a belt under their thighs, which they fasten
to their foreheads, and carry them hundreds of leagues
if they have no canoes. Other nations abandon their
prisoners in the woods, leaving them what they can to
subsist upon, beyond which, these miserable wretches
must seek in the forest the rest of their subsistence,
and that wherewith to dress their wounds. Some after
having been out some months have returned, while
others have perished of misery. They thus regard a
wounded man or a prisoner as a dead man.

Until they return to their villages, their prisoners are
well treated, and without ill temper. When a party
arrives, those who compose it, are all in file, one after
another, as on their departure. He who carries the
scalps is at the head. They are suspended along a pole.
Then come the prisoners, with a chichiquoi in hand
singing, although they do it unwillingly. All the warriors are silent. He who carries the pole of scalps then
first makes as many cries as they have lost men. It is
a doleful cry, and ends in a falling tone of voice, after
which he makes as many sharp cries as they have
scalps and prisoners, and a general cry terminates the

count. They recommence this again until they come to the chief's cabin. We can well imagine with what eagerness the young people, the women and the children run to meet them. The most active take the pole to carry to the chief, as if to announce to him the good news. Others seize hold of the prisoners, and each one endeavors to lead them to the chief's cabin. They are lucky if they have good legs, for they are assailed by a cloud of stones and with blows of clubs, and in this way alone they can have any advantage. All are in confusion except the warriors who remain tranquil, and continue their march as in a procession. If some one of the prisoners has the misfortune to fall, he is still worse treated, especially if he cries out, because this amuses them. It is extraordinary that they do not all get murdered in reaching the cabin, where all the chiefs and ancients are assembled.

He who conducts the war party, relates his journey and the expedition, gives justice to each one, and makes the eulogy of his warriors by mentioning their actions, after which he presents the prisoners to the assembly, when each in his turn must dance. We may well imagine that they do not do this willingly, especially if they are Europeans. But the Indian prisoners do not need to be urged, and this gives them an occasion to recount their bravery. This ceremony ended, the war chief disposes of the scalps and prisoners according to the destination previously agreed upon. Among the Iroquois, a prisoner is commonly des-

tined to replace some person deceased, by occupying
his place in the family. The whole nation regard him
as one of their members, and the new relatives take off
the collar of slavery. If the family do not wish to
adopt him, and say that they are too much afflicted to
think of replacing the dead, they give up the prisoner
to the young people to amuse themselves with. This
is an irrevocable decree, and the unfortunate wretch is
burned. We will not go into the details of this horrid
ceremony, which we find in all the authors. Happily
these events have become somewhat more rare. With
other nations the prisoners have more to complain of,
because they are regarded as their dogs, and they kill
them without consequences in their drunken moments,
and in times of scarcity, when they have no more scru-
ple at eating them than they would a beast. If a prisoner is so fortunate as to marry among these nations,
his family does not enjoy any considerations, and he is
exposed to all kinds of drudgery that they can invent.
Some are so lucky as to find kind Indians, with whom
they do not lead a hard and perilous life, especially if
they take care to keep away from drinking parties, by
taking these times to go out hunting.

Oftentimes when the conquerors have lost some chief
of great distinction, it is almost impossible to prevent
them from sacrificing some of their prisoners to the
manes of the dead. It is then, when to satisfy their
manes, that they eat a prisoner for ceremony. We
ought, however, to feel assured that they only taste

human meat with repugnance.   We have seen young people vomit more than once, and it is only by bravado, and by hardening the heart, that they sometimes get toughened to such a diet.

It is certain that the best way Europeans can take to fight the Indians is to corner them into some narrow passage, and march on them at full run, with bayonets fixed, for the troop which should amuse itself with firing would be soon beaten, on account of the accuracy of their fire.   If unfortunately they should disband they would be certainly destroyed, by their activity in attacking with hatchets and lances.[1]

Although the Indians have but little knowledge, they are, however, often found with a quick and brilliant spirit and much adroitness.   There are many who are very stupid, but is not this so among our own peasantry? The Indians have a strong memory. When any one has any thing to sell to them, they should take great care about lying to them, and it is always prudent to reserve a back door to guard against contrary events; in short, to make them see that you have not deceived them.   They are naturally so quiet, that they cannot conceive why we talk so much, and are always surprised at seeing us raise our tone of voice in our disputes.   They say that we then lose our spirit.

---

[1] The reflections upon warfare with Indians &c., which we find at the end of the relation of the expedition of Gen. Bouquet, against the Indians of Ohio, in 1764, merits a reference. The principles laid down by that author do not differ from those of M. Pouchot, but they have the advantage of being better developed.— *Note in Original.*

We have said that to gain their friendship, and many are in fact capable of showing a decided preference for some one, it is necessary to be generous. It is not, however, the quantity that we give them, which gains this reputation, and it passes for liberal or miserly, according to the way in which it is done. For instance, in giving them brandy to drink; if you present them with a large goblet half full, it is villainous, but if you offer a small one, providing that it is full, they are satisfied. If you offer them bread, it should be a whole loaf. A half loaf, although much larger, would make them say that you wanted to kill them by starving, and this alone might serve to bring the antipathies of a whole nation against a commandant. When we make them presents, it is best to begin by giving them what they least desire, because if they make some further request you will be able to grant it to them, which will serve to exalt your generosity.

Brandy is without doubt, the thing of all others that the Indians love the best. Every thing depends upon the manner of leading them in the proper way to drink or to trade. It is a means for attracting whole nations, and has become an object of a too great commerce, and we should be able to draw better parties upon some occasions. Although they would not now consent to be deprived of this pernicious liquor they are nevertheless very much ashamed of having become accustomed to it, and regard its use as the principal cause of their ruin.

With some minor differences, the Indians of this continent all resemble one another. We observe only that those who frequent the European colonies, are more tractable and intelligent. They designate their relations among themselves, and their superiority, by the terms of parent, uncle, nephew, cousins, &c. The Outaouais and the Abenakis call the Iroquois their uncles. The latter regard them as nephews, which indicates the great antiquity of this nation. We may find another proof in the names of many places, as *Ohio*, which signifies a fine river; *Theaogen*, the confluence of two rivers; *Schenatar*,[1] *Niagara*, and other names of places in parts more distant, which are all words in the Iroquois language. The Indians in speaking to the English, give them the appellation of Brothers, and to the French that of Fathers, to show that the latter visited them first, and that they should allow their children to want for nothing. When they wish to designate a whole nation, they call the English *Saganach*, the French *Mistigouch* and the Indians *Michinabé*. They designate the French officers by the name of *Onontio*, that is to say, Mountain, because one of the first whom they knew was called *Mount-Magny*.[2] Then

---

[1] This is the name of the city of *Orange*, situated upon the Hudson River in the province of New York.— *Note in Original.*

Evidently intended for *Schenectady* on the Mohawk.— ED.

[2] The Chevalier de Mount-Magny succeeded Champlain in 1636. He was the second governor of New France, and the first who had the glory of pacifying the Indian nations of the country, and of making a treaty with the Iroquois.— *Note in Original.*

by allusion they call the king of France the *Great Mountain*, *Onontio-Goa*, and the king of England, the Great Belt.

———

Addition upon the Number of Indians in North America.

Had the early travelers given us an exact account of the population of the Indians upon this continent, and had those who followed taken the same care, we might judge of the gradual diminution that has taken place. But this aid failing us, we are reduced to imperfect notions and vague reports. The result is not less afflicting to humanity.

When Champlain laid the first foundations of the French colony of Canada, several considerable nations whose names are now scarcely known, occupied this country. The language of the Algonquins, still used by several savage hordes, has alone preserved the memory of this great nation. The Hurons no longer form a people. These faithful and powerful allies of the French, after being scattered, have taken refuge in two villages remote from each other, the first near Quebec,[1] and the other at the extremity of the lakes. The Outaouais, formerly very numerous, now occupy only three villages, and the Poutéouatamis two. We now find no traces of the Bersiamiamites, the Papina-

———

[1] At Lorette, nine miles from Quebec.— ED.

chiois, the Montagnez, the Amikonés, the Attikamégues,
&c. These latter were surrounded by several other
tribes who extended to the environs of Lake St. John,
and to the lakes Mistassins and Némiscau. All have
been destroyed, chiefly in wars with the Iroquois.
The latter who were so formidable, and who could put
in the field at the end of the last century seven thousand five hundred warriors, can now scarcely assemble
fifteen hundred.

The eastern nations have suffered a diminution still
more sensible. Formerly they constituted, so to speak,
but one people, known to the French under the general
name of *Abenakis*. Their habitations were scattered
over that vast country which extends from the River
St. Lawrence, and following the Apalachian range as
far as to the southern extremity of the Carolinas. Although separated into many tribes, they spoke the
same language. The portion established near the
coast, lived only by fishing, and the rest by the chase.

In proportion as the English colonies increased, these
Indians have retired into the interior of the country
without ceding, as the English have pretended, the
country which they were forced to abandon. They
never had an idea of what we call *selling by contract*, or
ceding by treaty. The various hordes of this nation who
were fixed in Acadia or its environs, were distinguished under the name of *Abenakis, Etchemins, Souri-
quois, Mickmack*, &c. After the founding of New Hali-
fax, they made war against the English, who destroyed

33

almost all of them.   There are scarcely left more than
enough to form a few villages, which together might
have a thousand warriors.

The largest of the *Abenakis* tribe, remaining beyond
the Apalachian mountains is that of the Loups, whom
the English call *Delawares*.   They inhabit the banks of
the Ohio, where they reckoned eighteen hundred combatants at the close of the last war.   But this number
must be now greatly reduced by the losses they encountered in 1763–4, when they undertook to raise all
the Indians of the continent against the English.

The other nations who entered into this league,
chiefly resided upon the great lakes of Canada, and
near the rivers that flow into them.   Their loss was
much less considerable.   With the exception of the
Outagamis and the Missisakes, they are actually reduced to a very small number of men.

The Indians of the north and north-west, having but
little communication with Europeans, are but little
known.   We know only that the Scioux, the Christi-
naux and the Assiniboels are still quite numerous.
Although the Eskimaux and the other people of Lab-
rador, have some relations of trade with the English,
we are still ignorant of their population.   According
to the reports of the latter, about a thousand men and
as many women came annually in canoes to fort Nel-
son or York, to trade their peltries.

We know the names of a great number of people of
Louisiana, but this is almost all we do know.   They

have not ceased to vanish, if we may so speak, since the French have been established among them. In the space of only twenty-five years, their loss has been immense. We may be able to judge with some certainty by the excellent memoir, which M. de Bienville, governor of the French colony has made upon these regions.[1]

He therein mentions more than fifty nations, who before the year 1700 could put on foot 54,550 men. Twenty-five years after, they were reduced to 24,260. Many tribes who had formerly four, five and even six hundred combatants, had then only thirty, forty or fifty. Since this latter period, the most powerful have again suffered great diminution. The Chactas, who before the establishment of the French, had twenty thousand warriors, at the time of the enumeration of M. de Bienville had eight thousand, and now scarcely number four thousand. The Chicachas, the most formidable enemies of the French colonies, appear to be as numerous as the Chactas, but they should not actually be compared with them.[2]

From these details we may conclude with M. Buffon, that the most numerous nations in America, are reduced down to three or four thousand persons. He is

---

[1] This memoir is entitled *Le Cours du Mississipi, ou les Sauvages de la Louisiane, leur nombre & le commerce qu'on peut faire avec eux*, and is found printed in the journal of Trevoux, in the month of March, 1727.— *Note in Original.*

[2] A recent author only gives the Chicachas 750 warriors.— *Ib.*

persuaded, with reason, "that we may state without
fear of error, that in a single city like Paris,[1] there are
more men than there are Indians in all that part of
North America included between the Atlantic and the
Pacific, and from the Gulf of Mexico to the Polar seas,
although this extent of country is much greater than
that of the whole of Europe."[2]

This rapid diminution of the Indian nations may
be attributed, 1st, To the immoderate use of brandy;

---

[1] Supposing this city to embrace six or seven hundred thousand
souls.— *Note in Original*.

In a paper on the present state of the Northern Indians prepared
by Sir William Johnson in the fall of 1763, he gives a summary which
we condense in the following table.

	Men.		Men.
Mohawks,	160	Powtenatamis, near De-	
Oneidas,	250	troit,	150
Tuscaroras,	140	near St. Joseph,	200
Onondagas,	150	Ottawas near Detroit,	300
Cayugas,	200	near Michilimacinac,	250
Senecas,	1,050	near St. Joseph,	150
Oswegatchies,	80	Chipeweighs near De-	
Nanticokes,		troit,	320
Conoys,	200	near Michmck,	400
Tutecoes,		Meynomenys,	110
Saponeys, &c.,		Folsavoins,	110
Caghnawagas,	300	Puans,	360
Canassadagas,		Sakis,	300
Arudacks,	150	Foxes,	320
Algonqins,		Twightwees,	230
Abenaquis,	100	Kickapous,	180
Skaghquanoghronos,	40	Mascoutens,	90
Hurons,	40	Piankashaws,	100
Shawanese,	300	Wawiaghtonons,	200
Delawares,	600	Ottawaws, Chipeweighs,	
Wiandots, &c.,	200	&c.	4,000
Wiandots or Hurons,	250		
Total,			11,980

Not included in the above the Illinois, Scioux and some other
western tribes. Of these 3,960 belonged to the Iroquois confederacy,
and 2,800 to that of the Ottawas.—ED.

[2] *Hist. Nat.*, tom. v. p. 176, ed. in 12.—*Ib.*

2d, To the contagion of the small pox;[1] 3d, To the wars that the arrival of Europeans have occasioned; 4th. To the custom of replacing the dead by prisoners, which throws all these people into a state of continual war. Man there appears placed as the famous Hobbs has pretended,—and does not their conduct still justify the thought of that writer, who defines man as a vigorous child who knows his strength? In fact the Indian abuses himself, because he feels too much. He yields without difficulty to the impulses of vengeance, and raises the cry of arms, which he always takes to destroy, and never to acquire or to preserve. His appetite is tyrannical and his wants urgent. Both have been multiplied since the discovery of the new world. To satisfy these, he has forgotten his dearest interests, and has become the instrument of hatred between two powerful rivals, as also that of his own destruction.

APPROBATION.

I have read the work entitled, *Mémoires sur la dernière guerre de l'Amérique Septentrionale, &c.*, and I have found nothing which ought to prevent its printing.

At Yverdon, the 20th of December, 1780.

E. BERTRAND, *Censor.*

---

[1] To this epidemic we may add the most terrible of all, the Plague. In 1704 a king's vessel brought it to Mobile, where it destroyed two considerable nations, called the great and the little Thomés, &c.—*Note in Original.*

APPENDIX.

Note to Vol. i, Page 87.

LETTER FROM GENERAL WEBB TO COLONEL MONROE.

FORT EDWARD, *August* 4, 12 at noon.

SIR: I am directed by General Webb to acknowledge the receipt of three of your letters bearing date nine o'clock yesterday morning, and one about six in the evening, by the rangers, which are the only men that have got in here, except two yesterday morning with your first, acquainting him that the enemy were in sight. He has ordered me to acquaint you he does not think it prudent, (as you know his strength at this place), to attempt a junction, or to assist you, till reinforced by the militia of the colonies, for the immediate march of which, repeated expresses have been sent. One of our scouts brought in a Canadian prisoner last night, from the investing party, which is very large, and have possessed all the grounds five miles on this side of Fort William Henry. The number of the enemy is very considerable, the prisoners say, eleven thousand, and have a large train of artillery with mortars, and were to open their batteries this day. The general thought proper to send you this intelligence, that in case he should be so unfortunate from the delays of the militia, not to have it in his power to give you timely assistance, you might be able to make the best terms left in your power. The bearer is a sergeant of the Connecticut forces, and if he is happy enough to get in will bring advices from you. We keep continual scouts going to endeavor to bring intelligence from you. I am sir, with the heartiest and most anxious wishes for your welfare, your most obedient, humble servant,

C. BARTRAM, Aid-de-Camp.

To Col. Monroe, or officer commanding at Fort William Henry.

Note to Vol. i, Page 219.

Monument to Montcalm.

The following correspondence was had with reference to the Inscription in memory of Montcalm:

" To the Right Hon. Wm. Pitt.

SIR: The honors paid during your ministry, to the memory of Mr. Wolfe, give me room to hope that you will not disapprove of the grateful efforts made by the French troops to perpetuate the memory of the Marquis de Montcalm. The corpse of that general who was honored with the regret of your nation, is buried at Quebec. I have the honor to send you an epitaph, which the Academy of Inscriptions and Belles Lettres have wrote for him; and I would beg the favor of you, sir, to read it over, and if there be nothing improper in it, to procure me a permission to send it to Quebec, engraved in marble, to be put over the Marquis de Montcalm's tomb. If this permission should be granted, may I presume, sir, to entreat the honor of a line to acquaint me with it, and at the same time to send me a passport, that engraved marble may be received on board an English vessel, and that Mr. Murray, Governor of Quebec, may give leave to have it put up in the Ursuline Church. I ask pardon, sir, for taking off your attention, even for a moment, from your important concerns; but to endeavor to immortalize great men and illustrious citizens, is to do honor to you.　　　　　I am, &c.,

　　　　　　　　　　　　　　BOUGAINVILLE."

PARIS, *March 25th,* 1761.

' REPLY OF MR. PITT.

SIR: It is a real satisfaction to me to send you the king's consent on such an interesting subject, as the very handsome epitaph drawn by the Academy of Inscriptions at Paris, for the Marquis de Montcalm, which is desired to be sent to Quebec, engraved on marble, to be set up on the tomb of that illustrious warrior. The whole sentiments expressed in the desire to pay this tribute to the memory of their general, by the French troops who served in Canada, and who saw him fall at their head, in a manner worthy of him and worthy of them, cannot be too much applauded.

I shall take pleasure sir, in facilitating a design so full of respect to the deceased, and as soon as I am informed of the measures taken for embarking the marble, I shall immediately give the passport you desire, and send orders to the governor of Canada for its reception.

As to the rest, be assured, sir, that I have a just sense of the obliging things said to me in the letter with which you honored me, and that I think it a singular happiness to have an opportunity to express those sentiments of distinguished esteem and consideration with which I have the honor to be, &c.,

W. Pitt.

April 10, 1761.

———

General Montcalm's Epitaph.

HIC JACET.

Utroque in orbe æternùm Victurus
Ludovicus Josephus de Montcalm Gozon,
Marchio Sancti Verani, Baro Gabriaci,
Ordinis Sancti Ludovici, Commendator,
Legatus Generalis Exercituum Gallicorum.
Egregius et Cives et Miles,
Nullius Rei appetens, præterquam veræ laudis,
Ingenio felici et litteris exculto,
Omnes Militiæ gradus per continua decora emensus,
Omnium belli Artium, temporum, discriminum
gnarus
In Italiâ, in Bohemiâ, in Germaniâ,
Dux Industrius;
Mandata sibi, ita semper gerens, ut majoribus
par haberetur.
Jam claris periculis,
Ad tutandum Canadensem Provinciam missus
Parvâ Militûm manu, Hostium copias, non semel
repulit:
Propugnacula cepit viris armisque, instructissima.
Algoris, Inediæ, vigilarum, laboris patiens,
Suis unicè prospiciens, immemor sui,
Hostis acer, Victor Mansuetus.
Fortunam virtute, virium inopiam, peritiâ
Et celeritate, compensavit.
Imminens Coloniæ Fatum et consilio et manu per
quadriennium sustinuit.
Tandem ingentem exercitum Duce strenuo et
audaci,
Classemque omni bellorum mole gravem,
Multiplici prudentiâ, diù ludificatus,

Vi pertractus ad dimicandum,
In primâ acie, in primo conflictu, vulneratus,
Religioni, quam semper coluerat, innitens,
Magno suorum desiderio, nec sine hostium
mœrore extinctus est.
Die XIV Septem. A. D. M.DCC.LIX.
Ætat. XLVIII.
Mortales optimi Ducis exuvias, in excavatâ humo,
Quàm Globus bellicus decidens, disiliensque
defoderat,
Galli lugentes deposuerunt
Et generosæ Hostium fidei commendârunt.

[TRANSLATION.]

HERE LIETH,

In either Hemisphere to live for ever,
LEWIS JOSEPH DE MONTCALM GOZON,
Marquis of St. Veran, Baron of Gabriac,
Commendatory of the Order of St. Lewis,
Lieutenant General of the French Army. —
Not less an excellent Citizen than Soldier;
Who knew no desire but that of true Glory.
Happy in a Natural Genius, improved by Literature;
Having gone through the several Steps of Military Honors
With an uninterrupted lustre,
Skilled in all the Arts of War,
The juncture of the times, and the crisis of danger:
In Italy, in Bohemia, in Germany,
An indefatigable General:
He so discharged his important trust;
That he seemed always equal to still greater.
At length grown bright with Perils,
Sent to secure the Province of Canada
With a handful of Men,
He more than once repulsed the Enemy's Forces,
And made himself Master of their Forts
Replete with Troops and Ammunition.
Inured to Cold, Hunger, Watching and Labours,
Unmindful of himself,
He had no sensation, but for his Soldiers:
An Enemy with the fiercest Impetuosity:

34

A Victor with the tenderest Humanity
Adverse Fortune he compensated with Valour;
The want of Strength, with Skill and Activity;
And, with his Counsel and Support
For Four Years protracted the impending
Fate of the Colony. —
Having with various Artifices
Long baffled a Great Army,
Headed by an expert and Intrepid Commander,
And a Fleet furnished with all warlike stores;
Compelled at length to an Engagement,
He fell, in the first rank, in the first onset, warm with those hopes
of Religion which he had always cherish'd —
To the inexpressible loss of his own Army,
And not without the regret of the Enemy's —
XIV. September, A. D. M.DCC.LIX.
Of his Age XLVIII.
His weeping Countrymen
Deposited the remains of their Excellent General in a Grave
Which a fallen Bomb in bursting had excavated for him,
Recommending them to the general Faith of their Enemies.

INDEX.

Lightning Source UK Ltd.
Milton Keynes UK
UKHW051207190123
415622UK00013B/728

9 789354 489846